M.S. Swaminathan in Conversation with Nitya Rao

M.S. Swaminathan

in conversation

with Nitya Rao

From Reflections on My Life to the Ethics and Politics of Science

ACADEMIC FOUNDATION
NEW DELHI

www.academicfoundation.org

First published in 2015
by

ACADEMIC FOUNDATION
4772-73 / 23 Bharat Ram Road, (23 Ansari Road),
Darya Ganj, New Delhi - 110 002 (India).
Phones : 23245001 / 02 / 03 / 04.
Fax : +91-11-23245005.
E-mail : books@academicfoundation.com
www.academicfoundation.org

in association with
M.S. Swaminathan Research Foundation, Chennai.

Photographs courtesy: M.S. Swaminathan Research Foundation, Chennai.

Cataloging in Publication Data--DK
Courtesy: D.K. Agencies (P) Ltd. <docinfo@dkagencies.com>

Swaminathan, M. S. (Monkombu Sambasivan), author.
M.S. Swaminathan in conversation with Nitya Rao : from reflections on my life to the ethics and politics of science / edited by Nitya Rao.
pages cm
Includes bibliographical references (pages).
ISBN 9789332701861

1. Swaminathan, M. S. (Monkombu Sambasivan)--Interviews. 2. Plant geneticists--India--Biography. 3. Green Revolution--India. 4. Agriculture--Moral and ethical aspects--India. 5. Agriculture and state--India. I. Rao, Nitya, editor. II. Title.

DDC 576.5092 23

Typeset by Italics India, New Delhi.

Printed and bound by The Book Mint, New Delhi.
www.thebookmint.in

Contents

Foreword. 7

Introduction 11

PART I
Reflections on My Life

Introduction 15

1. Putting People First 19
2. Recognising Women's Contributions. 27
3. Education, Information and Social Mobilisation 33
4. Upholding Human and National Dignity 39
5. Motivating and Managing People 45
6. Science in the Service of Society 55
7. Dealing with Criticism 61
8. Dealing with the State: Issues of Governance. 67
9. Contextual Embeddedness and Cultural Diversity 73
10. Maintaining High Ethical Standards 77
11. Unfinished Agendas 81
12. Conclusions: The Making of a Leader 83

PART II
The Ethics and Politics of Science

Introduction 89

1. From Ship to Mouth to Right to Food: A 60-Year Journey 93

2. Grain Mountains and Hungry Millions: The Reality of Agrarian Distress 119

3. The Politics and Economics of Seeds 129

4. Integrated Planning and Management of Resources 147

5. Social, Demographic and Gender Dimensions of Science and Technology 169

6. Agricultural Research Strategies 187

7. Science and Public Policy 197

Reflections 211

Afterword 213

References 215

References to People. 217

Annex 1: Farewell Statement by Prof M.S. Swaminathan: 22 March 2013. 221

M.S. Swaminathan: Highlights of Career 225

Foreword[1]

At a recent gathering in Delhi, two of the most eminent men in India occupied the stage—Dr M.S. Swaminathan, the agricultural scientist with a social mission and Dr Karan Singh, scholar of Indian religion and culture, diplomat and statesman. The occasion was the launch of a very readable little book of conversations with Dr Swaminathan by his scholar-daughter Nitya Rao (Part I of the present publication) by Karan Singh, and I was to introduce it. I noticed that both of them were in grey safari suits.

Relaxing in my chair, and observing them, I began to muse on the colour grey. The *raja*-turned-*pandit* and the *pandit*-turned-*kisan* are rarely seen in attire other than grey or grey-blue safari suits. Why did they both choose this colour? Was it not an uninspiring, unremarkable colour with no specific character of its own? What does grey signify?

Most persons on the stage and in the audience, with fine heads of salt and pepper, looked wise and eminent. And made me think—loud, needless to say—on the French phrase *eminence grise*, or grey eminence.

Why should eminence be described in that most boring of all colours? Why, leaving all the vivid colours of the rainbow, should grey, that drab shade of black resisting white, be joined to eminence? Or, to be very literal, is the phrase about salt hair, trying in vain, to look salt-and-pepper, on the eminent head? Or to the larger fact that as eminence ages or age turns eminent, it inclines it to grey rather than brightly coloured clothes, grey woollens, grey gloves, grey scarves and, if only they existed, to grey footwear? Perhaps.

---

1. Address delivered by Gopal Krishna Gandhi on 6 September 2013 at the release function of the booklet M.S. Swaminathan in Conversation with Nitya Rao which comprises Part 1 of the present volume. Adapted from "Advisers, Not Courtiers", *Hindustan Times*, 6 September 2013.

But I think there is another, more subtle reason for the coupling of grey to eminence: Grey is a nowhere colour. Eminence is a no-win status.

Grey in fact is not a colour as much as the shadow of colours in a nervous mix. But if one were to call it a colour and invest 'meaning' in it, grey would be the colour of hope in retreat, of aspiration in decline, of wry experience being superseded by spry expertise.

Grey is the colour of ash. And ash is about what was.

Grey is the colour of smoke. And smoke is about what is no more.

Grey is the colour of aspiration dusted over by the rebuff of neglect.

Pride in experience turns ashen before the hubris of cock-sureness. It turns smokey before myopia.

Grey eminence is more grey than eminent—not so weak as to have to sit down when exhausted, not so strong as to be able to jump to attention at the sound of power's bugles. Grey eminence is as worried as it is wise; but such is its two-colour tone culture of self-restraint, that it is happier to suggest than to prescribe, to wish, to hope, to urge and even, at times, to lend its signature to the idiom of protest. Grey eminence can have the impulse to mail its fist, but is curbed by obligations to stay its hand. It is thoughtful in a world of calculations, knowledgeable in times of self-willed ignorance. Grey eminence is respected but it knows and rues the fact that if eminence is respected, prominence is applauded.

Eminence is owned. Prominence is borrowed.

Eminence is co-extensive with life. Prominence is co-terminous with influence.

There have been times, though, when the seemingly impossible has happened—eminence has managed to get and keep some prominence and prominence has actually looked eminent. And that is what has happened with Karan Singh and Swaminathan. They have managed, almost as if by a miracle, to be both eminent and prominent.

But while their eminence is theirs for all time, their prominence loves truancy. When Karan Singh or Swaminathan join, as nominees for the President of India, the council of the states, the Rajya Sabha, more than another MP takes his seat in that august hall. A social philosopher and a wise man comes to its deliberations. But as Karan Singh said of Swaminathan at that book event, Swaminathan's voice is washed way in the torrents that flood the Parliament's time away.

Eminence counsels, prominence prescribes.

Eminence draws disciples. Prominence acquires courtiers.

Counsel can combine the features of an exhortation which is persuasive, an expostulation which is dissuasive, and a warning that can be an admonitory, making the person giving it an amalgam of adviser, prompter, monitor, mentor, critic, guide, teacher. But, above all, a counsellor.

Every age has seen counsellors heard, respected, placed on a side. Every age has seen courtiers hold smiles like garlands, bowing pick-thanks, rise to a brief nod by power.

Counsellors are not the most convenient persons to have around, but they are needed. Courtiers are not needed, they are convenient to have around.

Unjust and unwise wars have been fought against 'grey' counsel. Dishonourable treaties of peace have been secured by 'coloured' counsel.

Famines have been brought upon hapless people by ignoring of 'grey' counsel and, equally, droughts have been fought with the help of timely counsel given by 'grey' sagacities.

Counsellors of the state have minds; they also have consciences. That is their strength, their signature.

Do states have a mind?

They do; but they also have compulsions.

States need to balance things—the necessary with the expedient, the desirable with the prudent, the short-term with the mid-term and both with the long-term.

Counsellors do not need to balance anything, for they are themselves, like the colour grey, balanced already between agelessness and ageing, inevitability and volition, disappointment and contentment, hope and resignation.

Nitya Rao's publication on her father ends with a brief note on the qualities of a leader. It is insightful. Grey does not figure in it but it shows how convictions, bravely held and powerfully expressed, can turn grey from a colour to be lived with to a tone to be lived by.

—Gopalkrishna Gandhi
Former administrator, Diplomat and Governor

Introduction

This book consists of two parts, both written at different times in different settings, and also with different purposes. They are not sequential, yet belong together.

While mainly recognised for the Green Revolution, I started my conversations with M.S. Swaminathan, who I knew as someone with a wealth of rich and diverse experiences, going far beyond genetics or even science per se. I wanted to capture the richness and nuances of his insights and emotions over a long career that spans the first six decades of Indian Independence.

Part I is more biographical in nature. A large number of experiences throughout his life are not only recorded, but discussed thematically; they are not necessarily presented in chronological order. The various influences leading up to each experience or coming out of it are also recorded; yet it is ultimately the story of his life, and how he reacted to different situations and challenges. The most significant stretch in this part does indeed, relates to the Green Revolution years, where the documentation is sweeping in its range, but succinct in its presentation, capturing a very significant and formative period in his life. It is in this sense that Part I can be described as a life story, looked back upon from the perspective of age.

Part II, however, is entirely different in nature. It is more reflective biographical, and concerned with issues which had to be confronted in the course of his career. In this part, he examines how politics influences and determines the course of agricultural development; how different ethical stances, often in conflict, come into play. This is not just in the past, but equally in the present, though seen now from and through the perspective of age, reflecting with mature wisdom on experiences long gone. It is also more driven by the questions I raised, pressing for his views on various issues. While in Part I, I also raised questions, these were more to elucidate and strengthen the description, and draw out inferences. In Part II, the questions were more directed towards understanding the man himself, as well as the meaning, context and relationships between the various experiences unveiled. For example, one can see the emergence of a changing perspective over the years—one that is more oriented towards agriculture and production in the early years, but shows greater inclination towards farmers' understanding and needs in the latter years.

In that sense, the two are complementary—the first tells the story, the second reflects on implications of the story. That is why I wanted to present the two together—they uphold two sides of the same story—the first about his life, and the second about his thoughts on life. Together perhaps they tell the full story—or so I hope.

I would like to acknowledge the many people who have contributed to this book. First of all, the subject, my father Prof M.S. Swaminathan, for his time and patience in both responding to my initial questions and later to requests for clarifications; and to my mother, Mina Swaminathan, for her contributions to the conversations, but also to the editing of the original manuscript. There are many people who offered their photographs—some of which have been used in this book. I would specifically like to thank Amit Mitra, Rajiv Krishnamurthy, Israel Oliver King and the MSSRF photo library for their generosity. Dilhara Begum helped transcribe the recordings, which facilitated the writing of this book. Innumerable friends and relatives have supported this project, and I am grateful to all of them for their encouragement and feedback.

PART I

Reflections on My Life

Introduction

1. Putting People First
2. Recognising Women's Contributions
3. Education, Information and Social Mobilisation
4. Upholding Human and National Dignity
5. Motivating and Managing People
6. Science in the Service of Society
7. Dealing with Criticism
8. Dealing with the State: Issues of Governance
9. Contextual Embeddedness and Cultural Diversity
10. Maintaining High Ethical Standards
11. Unfinished Agendas
12. Conclusions: The Making of a Leader

Introduction

My parents walked with the cortege when Gandhiji died. He was a postgraduate student at the Indian Agricultural Research Institute (IARI), and she was still at school—they had not yet met. He had seen Gandhiji from close quarters; she had never had the opportunity to do so. He had grown up in a small town and rural India, she in the urban metros. Yet they belong to a generation that was driven by a tremendous love for the nation and a strong sense of patriotism. They met in Cambridge a few years later. After their marriage in 1955, they followed different career paths. Despite their divergent interests and trajectories, there has always been a strong sense of partnership and mutual support, of shared values and philosophies, emerging from a desire to serve the country, especially the disadvantaged. Their respect and love for each other makes them bond, supporting each other in times of joy and grief, success and adversity. Their lives have been truly complementary.

In our home, Amma was discipline incarnate, but also full of creativity, play and adventure, while Appa's worst scolding took the form of telling us that we wouldn't be given chocolates if we were naughty! Despite his busy schedule, in our childhood, he always made time for our Sunday 'oil-baths' and 'made-up, bed-time' stories, as well as the full-day picnics organised by Amma. So when he was travelling, she was left with the additional burden of coping with our tantrums. I am told that when I was little and couldn't yet read, I would eat the postcards he wrote to me. She would raise her voice; he was always calm. His gentle personality and trusting nature extended beyond the home; when troubled by conflict and wrongdoing, he found it difficult to handle directly, and she had to pitch in.

As children, we went regularly not only to the labs at IARI, but also to villages and farmer's fields. Yet we three sisters were never directed on what we should do, but given every freedom to grow and pursue our own interests, which we have done, each in our own way. Seeing parents over-protective of their children today, I am amazed that they encouraged my interest in rural development when I was still a teenager at Delhi University, not objecting to my spending the summer holidays in rural Bihar, Rajasthan and Uttarakhand in the early 1980s—a time when there were no mobile phones or easy forms of communication. I have since experimented with many things in my own life, from grass-roots organisation to activism in support of women's rights and advocacy, and now an academic career. Though unplanned, my career has moved in a direction that combines their diverse interests: gender relations and rural development.

Supported by my mother, my father started the M S Swaminathan Research Foundation (MSSRF) in 1988. I really wanted to know what drove them relentlessly for the last 25 years, despite adversities and problems. What was it that led them to take up this project, and sustain it, through arguments and differences of opinion, especially as the organisation has grown rapidly and often in ways they would not have chosen? My seeking answers to these questions led to the idea of this book. I had thought that I would get them to dialogue with each other and be the scribe. Yet this became too complex a project—one that I was unable to handle at this juncture.

This part therefore focuses primarily on the ideas and efforts of M.S. Swaminathan, bringing together insights on the human values and ethical principles that have been essential for realising his dream—that of securing human dignity through food sovereignty and security in India. Based on conversations with him over a period of two weeks in June-July 2013, this book seeks to engage with basic principles of life with means and ends. Personal integrity emerges as perhaps the most important value, giving him the strength to stand up for justice in support of the excluded and voiceless. It documents how personal and professional lessons were learned and imbibed through life's diverse experiences, from childhood through adulthood. Equally important is how these lessons were translated into practice, with grit and determination, often against serious odds. The combination of intellectual capacity with social commitment and non-negotiable moral standards is a mark of leadership par excellence, rarely matched in the country in recent decades.

In his life's work, his wife, Mina Swaminathan, has been a firm partner and collaborator at every stage. She regularly provided the 'social glue,' engaging creatively with the institutions he was leading, in particular IARI, International Rice Research Institute (IRRI) and MSSRF. In each, she organised a variety of social events and activities to build solidarity, 'interventions' that were not insignificant in supporting his characteristic style of leadership, and often did the first editing of his writing. At IARI, she hosted parties to felicitate students who successfully crossed certain milestones, as well as visiting scientists and dignitaries. They may have held opposite views during the day in meetings they attended, but would end up laughing and playing games together. So, while not a dialogue any more, I do bring in comments from her now and again. Most important, of course, is that as always, she has been the facilitator, making this book happen.

Rather than being arranged chronologically, this book highlights the underlying philosophy of M.S. Swaminathan's life and contributions, drawing on critical experiences that have shaped this process. In the form of short anecdotes and stories drawn from different periods of his life, these demonstrate the clarity of goals, vision and purpose, the continuity and strength of his convictions. Yet he is not rigid, but willing to discuss, share and learn, confronting problems as they arise, adapting to the social contexts in which he is functioning. Taking him as an exemplar of the idea of lifelong learning, the book highlights his immense respect for people of all social groups and a recognition that no one is too small to contribute to the collective production of knowledge.

1

Putting People First

A key principle for M.S. Swaminathan (MSS) is not to see people instrumentally, but as human beings with strengths and weaknesses, each having something to contribute to the collective good. He has experienced humility and encouragement first hand, seeing and learning from his father, his teachers, or indeed superiors, who gave him the freedom to work, rather than getting involved in petty jealousies. Be it drivers or cooks, students or colleagues, in India or abroad, he always treats them as people first, making them all remember him fondly. His immense faith in people has meant that, at times, he has been let down by some, yet in a majority of cases, this faith has paid off.

Secularism and the Equality of All People—Childhood Memories

I remember Gandhiji coming to our town, Kumbakonam. He used to stay in our hospital, because my father, a well-known doctor, was a Congress leader. In those days, in middle class families in Tamil Nadu and Kerala, boys also used to wear earrings and a chain. One day my mother told us, "He will ask for your chain and earrings, you must give them to him." I didn't understand fully at the time, but because my mother said so, when Gandhiji asked for the gold ornaments, we gave it to him. Next day, I asked her why he wanted them, and she said he would auction it and use the money for Harijan (Dalit) welfare, for helping those who don't have much. Gandhiji's principle of trusteeship has been one that I have followed in my own life. Whatever is surplus to your requirement, hold it as a trustee rather than as an owner and use it for the welfare of those who are less privileged. When I received the Borlaug award, I gave it to Mobile Creches; thereafter, I have donated all other awards too.

One of the Gandhiji's programmes was temple entry for the Harijans, and my father was actively associated with it. He must have played an important part in convincing the Maharaja of Travancore, because he was his personal doctor. So in those days, the priests wouldn't come to our house because they objected to Dalits coming and eating, sitting with us, and of course the temple entry movement. When his mother, my grandmother, died, no Brahmin priests would come to the house, so he went to Banaras to perform her last rites. He didn't care whether the priests came or not. My father's brother was different; he tried to make peace with them. My mother also wouldn't go so far, so slowly the priests were rehabilitated in the family.

These were formative years; they taught me the value of money, but more importantly, of being satisfied with what one has, rather than striving for huge surpluses as Gandhiji said, "There is enough in this world for everybody's need, but not enough for anybody's greed." Second and more importantly, it ingrained in me the principles of secularism and of fighting against injustice, always taking the side of the poor, and those denied an equal voice in society, whether small farmers or women. Dalits, muslims, everyone was equally welcome in our house.

Mina: On 14 August 1947, we sat up at night to hear Jawaharlal Nehru's famous "Tryst with Destiny" speech on the radio at midnight and see the fireworks and celebrations that followed. And then in January 1948, my parents had taken me one evening to the house of a colleague. All the kids were playing badminton in the garden. And suddenly at about 5 pm, the adults came out of the house and shouted, "Stop playing children, Gandhiji has been killed." We stopped playing at once and came and sat in front of the radio to hear the news. The house was not far from the place where he was shot, Birla House; the adults went there, but didn't allow us to go. But two days later we all went for the funeral. There were huge crowds of people, most had walked from the surrounding villages. The streets were packed—people standing on the walls, climbing on trees—that's how we saw the whole funeral procession. And I think one of my greatest regrets, as a great admirer of Gandhiji, has been that though I was in Delhi at that time, I never saw him alive.

In 1955, I met one of those who influenced me a lot in my teaching career, Ayesha Jacob, who was the head of St. Thomas' School at that time—what is called an 'aided school', a category where bulk of the expenses are borne by the government, though it is a private institution. The fees were very low and could attract all the children in the community, including those of low-level clerical and other government employees who lived in that area, as well as children of petty tradesmen who lived in Paharganj—the girls from these families all being first generation learners. When I saw this place, I decided this is where I wanted to work because it was for this community of children that I could do something. The school was located just next to the Bhangi Colony where Gandhiji had lived, and where he took his morning walks. In fact, a play which I did there later, for the Gandhi Centenary Year, was titled 'Gandhiji Walked Here'. Over 1000 students from classes 6 to 11 were involved; each given a segment of Gandhiji's life, from his days in South Africa till his death, to explore and dramatise using methods of creative drama, so they would understand the spirit and feeling of the text. The pageant went on for two hours and was a beautiful spectacle.

Learning and Practising Personal Humility

In 1947, just after I joined Indian Agricultural Research Institute (IARI) as a student, a friend of the family, S.Y. Krishnaswamy (formerly Collector of Kumbakonam), suggested that I should sit for the competitive examinations, as there was no future in agricultural research. I did, and to my surprise, was selected for the Indian Police Service (IPS). My uncle was delighted, saying that a bird in hand was worth two in the bush, and research would never bring me such an income. I was in a dilemma. Luckily, at about this time, in 1948, I got an offer of a Fellowship to the Agricultural University at Wageningen in Holland. This satisfied the family, and they agreed that I should accept it.

I went to Holland by a boat called *Jal Azad* in 1949. It was a small boat and a rough journey. There were larger P&O liners, but somehow due to a nationalistic spirit, I chose *Jal Azad*. I reached Holland and started my work on potatoes. There was an interesting event when I arrived at the station in Ede-Wageningen. There was hardly anybody else getting out there. I had a big box. An old gentleman was walking towards me. He said, "Are you Swaminathan?" I said, "Yes." "Hand over the bag to me; I came here to take you." Then he took me to his house and I found he was the Rector Magnificus! I felt so bad handing over the bag to him as if he was some porter. We had lunch and then he sent somebody with me to find accommodation. That was very nice of him.

I found a place in the house of a Mrs Maarseveen. She was a wonderful lady. I was a pure vegetarian at that time. She felt bad that I was just eating cheese and milk. Suddenly I found she was cooking vegetarian dishes, and she told me she had joined a cookery class to learn those dishes. I found these people to be very kind. I stayed for a year in Holland. Then I went to Cambridge in 1950 to complete my PhD at the Commonwealth Potato Collection. I continued my work on the tuber bearing solanum potatoes, which came from the Andean region. I got my PhD degree from Cambridge in two years.

My paper, published in the *American Potato Journal*, caught the eye of Prof G.H. Rieman and Prof D.C. Cooper, who found it very interesting and invited me to Wisconsin. I travelled by the *Queen Elizabeth*, which took seven days. It was very exciting to see the Statue of Liberty as one entered the New York Bay. I stayed for a year and helped develop the station at Sturgeon Bay, but then I had to take a decision. The University offered me a tenure track position as Assistant Professor in Genetics with a good salary. But I told President Fred that it was not my intention to stay abroad, but to equip myself to serve my country. I could have lived with comfort in the United States (US), but my intention was always to serve Indian agriculture. What I learnt from Cambridge and Wisconsin, however, was ways to articulate clear, goal-oriented research, and then develop a strategy to accomplish it. This helped me with my latter work with dwarf wheats in IARI, as I had developed a clear idea of the end point and how to reach it, surely and speedily.

I returned to India without any work. I was staying at home in Kumbakonam, helping my brother Krishnamurthy pack drugs in the new pharmaceutical venture he had started. At Aduthurai rice station near Kumbakonam, there was a function to mark Farmers' Day, and they invited me. There I met Dr N. Parthasarathy, my former teacher in Delhi. He asked what I was doing, and when he heard I was doing nothing, he asked me to come to Cuttack. There was a temporary job as part of the *indica-japonica* hybridisation programme, which involved transferring genes for fertiliser response from *japonica* to *indica*. I willingly agreed, as it was no fun sitting at home. So I went to Cuttack, and while there, some of my applications matured. The Union Public Service Commission (UPSC) selected me for the post of Assistant Cytogeneticist at IARI, and therefore I left for Delhi in October.

For the next 18 years I was at IARI. The Director, in my student days, was Dr J.N. Mukherjee, an eminent soil scientist who encouraged me very much. He was one of the few who asked me not to accept the IPS, but continue my research career. When I returned, Dr Pal had become the Director, I knew him well from my student days; he was then the Head of the Botany division. He too was very encouraging, not one of those who suffered from 'retrospective jealousy'. He gave me a free hand to work.

Family Life

My parents tell me they started their married life with a joint income of only ₹ 600-700 a month. But they were quite happy with simple living and so were we. Memories of my childhood are mostly of fun and games, picnics and holidays, puppet shows and Christmas parties. During the summer holidays, we would go to Kumbakonam to be with our grandparents and spend time with cousins, uncles and aunts, playing with cows in the large garden and visiting beautiful temples in the evenings. As we grew up, we developed our own interests, had our own friends, yet dinner was a time that we all came together to eat and share what we had done during the day. We had an Alsatian dog, Diana, who, not to be left out, insisted on eating with us, rather than separately.

When I first joined service in 1954 at Central Rice Research Institute (CRRI), Cuttack, and then at IARI, New Delhi, my starting salary was ₹ 450 per month, with a small reduction for pension contribution. In 1955, when Mina and I got married, we had to manage with this amount. The rent was ₹ 130 per month for a flat in Patel Nagar. Mina had also joined the Central Institute of Education that year for her BEd degree, so she could contribute nothing, and even after she got a job the pay of a teacher was only ₹ 200! Yet we could comfortably manage with this amount. In 1956, when I became a cytogeneticist, the salary went up to ₹ 700 per month. As the Director, IARI, my salary was ₹ 2,000-2,500. During the 1960s, we had to take care not only of the household expenses, but also the upbringing of three children. Yet we never felt we had to sacrifice the care and comfort of our children because of lack of money. In addition, I used to get ₹ 4,000-5,000 each year from our properties in Kerala.

Later when I became the Director General of Indian Council of Agricultural Research (ICAR), the salary was ₹ 3,500 per month, but it went down to ₹ 2,250 when I became, first Acting Deputy Chairman and later Member of the Planning Commission, because that was the allowance then for ministers of state. Although in these circumstances there was little possibility of saving money, there was enough to look after all our needs, because prices were very low in comparison to today. Our first priority was the children's education as we did not want them to feel handicapped because of lack of money. Our lifestyle was simple and expenditure restricted to essentials, like food and education. We travelled by cycle or bus, and got a car only in 1962.

It was only after I joined International Rice Research Institute (IRRI), that I could save some money to buy a house when we returned to India from the Philippines. Between 1970 and 2000, I received several prizes with substantial amounts in rupee terms. The very first award with cash was the Ramon Magsaysay Award for Community Leadership (1971), at that time 10,000 US dollars at an exchange rate of ₹ 7.50 per dollar. *The Hindustan Times* had an interesting article with the title "What will Swaminathan do with ₹ 75,000?" Today senior government employees and professionals earn more than this every month!

Mina: Balancing work with family has been a basic principle throughout my life, so as soon as my second daughter was born in 1961, I decided to go part-time, so that I could have more time for my young children, though I did have help, of course. But my part-time work was nearly full time, because I worked only half a day but packed all my work, or 80 per cent of it, into that half day. The employers were getting full time value for part-time payment! But I got the experience and managed to find time for my family. By 1963, when our youngest daughter was born, MSS was getting increasingly busy. Though he found time for the children, I too had to give a lot of time, organising multiple activities, as well as picnics and holidays when we could all be together, even if in a village or in one of the research institutes affiliated to ICAR.

Looking for Challenges, Not Power

In December 1981, Dr Clarence Grey, Chairman, Board of Trustees of the International Rice Research Institute, rang up and said he wanted to meet me. He came home for lunch, and informed that the IRRI Board had invited me to be the next Director General (DG). I told that I had not applied, but he insisted I was their first choice. I was tired of the Planning Commission. I had worked hard, the Sixth Plan had been finalised, and I wanted to go back to research. I told him I could not say yes or no without the consent of the Prime Minister (PM), Indira Gandhi.

I went to her secretary, P.C. Alexander. He said that she would never relieve me, so before meeting her I prepared a note on why I wanted to go. I got an appointment to meet the PM. She said, "You are indispensable, we can't spare you. You have done so much important work in the Planning Commission. Why do you want to quit now?" I said that the Plan was ready and approved. Now it was a question of implementation. She asked if I had made them a commitment. I said, "No. I have clearly told them that I will have to get the approval of the PM." I was chairing a number of committees at the time, so I said, "If you approve, I will hold on for four months till all the reports are ready. I can go in April. But I must give them some date, I can't keep them waiting." I also told her, "You said I am indispensable. So I must go." She asked if I was hurt. I said, "No. In fact I am elated that you consider me indispensable. I must go when I am wanted, not stay till I am not wanted." She smiled and repeated that, and then offered her good wishes. Alexander was anxious to know what happened. I said she had kindly agreed to my going and he was surprised.

I told Clarence Grey that I could join only in April, because of commitments that I needed to attend and could not leave overnight. He asked me to come for a visit to assure the staff that a new DG was indeed going to arrive. So Mina and I went there for a short visit. Leaving her work in Delhi and going to Los Banos was a very difficult and painful decision for her. But she enthusiastically endorsed my desire to take up the job, since she felt that this is what I wanted to do. Throughout her life, she has put her personal preferences aside for my sake, including our shift from Delhi to Chennai in 1989.

Mina: He asked me if I was ready to live abroad for several years, as he knew that I wanted to work only in India, and that probably I would be frustrated there without work. But, hard though it was for me to face that prospect, I had no hesitation in saying "Yes." In the event, those years proved productive, as well as a great learning experience, though in far different ways than I could have imagined. In the first year, I travelled up and down to Delhi, making sure the girls were okay, besides productively engaging with the domain of educational policy, joining the debates and discussions culminating in the National Education Policy, 1986, in which I wrote the chapter on Early Childhood Education, and then the NEP 1989, in which Anil Sadgopal and I included the demand for the right to education to be extended from birth to 6 years, as articulated in Article 45 of the Directive Principles.

2

Recognising Women's Contributions

MSS has been a consistent champion of women's rights and entitlements, introducing in the Sixth Five Year Plan, for the first time, a chapter on women and development. Despite some criticism from within the Planning Commission, he felt it is important to signal the centrality of women's contributions and a commitment to gender equality. As a member of the Rajya Sabha, he introduced the Women Farmers' Entitlement Bill in Parliament in 2011, calling for recognition of women as farmers, and as equals. The stories below give an insight into his deep faith in gender equality, attempting to advocate for women's equal recognition and rights, wherever he went, irrespective of how successful he was. While moved by a concern for women's tireless work and its invisibility, the strategies he has proposed have been empowering rather than welfarist, recognising women as thinking individuals, in control of their lives, not as receivers of doles and benefits. Deep down a concern for women, and their social invisibility, was already ingrained in me. After I completed my postgraduate diploma at Institute of Rural Management Anand (IRMA) in 1985, the first job I took was with Self Employed Women's Association (SEWA), a women's organisation.

Growing up in a Joint Family: The Invisibility of Women's Work

When I was young, we used to go to Moncompu during every vacation. I knew that the family was rich in terms of land ownership, but they were very simple, didn't flaunt their money, and one couldn't make out the difference between the rich and poor in Kerala, whether Christians, Muslim or Dalit. Kerala culture was also simple then, not like today, with dowry, gold and drinking. It was also an area where we could go for boating and swimming in the river. Since I was part of a joint family, during the vacation, 30-40 children used to be there and poor Krishna Anna's mother and Ratnam's mother (my aunts) used to make so many good things for us to eat. They only thought about ways to feed the boys and girls, totally sacrificing their own personal life for their families. My mother too used to spend hours cooking for the children. I used to admire them, but also felt sad that they are spending their life like this. However, one could see the joy they derived by ensuring that the children and others were well fed.

In the joint family system, all are equal and no distinction is made between one's own child and another's. In some ways, this provides an opportunity for more humanistic values, trying to help each other, especially when someone is in distress. In fact, in relation to the Vidarbha suicides nowadays, the family system which provided social protection appears to have totally broken down. I remember, in those days, one of my father's sisters was not so well off; so his elder brother took them to Wayanad, gave them some land and settled them there. Within the joint family, they would not let you down.

Mina: When I got married and met MSS' family, it was a big surprise to me—it was another world— the world from which I had come was quite different. It was a huge, extended, rural family, with its many branches. I had to get to know them all and it was a new experience, but I embraced this experience with great joy and enthusiasm. I wanted to learn all about it, to be a part of it. I thought it was wonderful that they loved me so much in spite of the fact that I was so different. None of my sisters-in-law, neither the brides nor the daughters of the family, had any education beyond school leaving. Immediately after leaving school, they had all been married off and after that, it was only and totally a domesticated life. They found it interesting to explore my life and I explored theirs, and we all became great friends.

Women in Rice Farming and the Bellagio Conference

When I joined IRRI in April 1982, I found that the institution was organising an Annual International Rice Conference for 1983. I suggested 'Women and Rice Farming' as the theme. There was some opposition and ill-informed questions and comments, such as 'What do women know?' 'Why should the conference focus on them?' 'Is this a kind of affirmative action?' I asked them, "Have you ever gone to a rice field and seen who is working there?" That was a turning point. The Asian Network of Women and Rice Farming was formed and the Ford Foundation agreed to fund it. Earlier, affirmative action was taken only in terms of counting how many trustees and staff members were women. It was only number crunching, the research or training programmes were not engendered. We started mainstreaming gender in the whole production process of agriculture. This was a lasting contribution not only to IRRI but also to the Consultive Group on International Agriculture Research (CGIAR).

The Rockefeller Foundation had representatives at the Women and Rice conference. They were so impressed that they decided to sponsor a meeting at Bellagio for the entire CGIAR network, most of which were gender blind institutions. I presented the Keynote Address and told them what we had done. That was a good meeting and a turning point also in CGIAR's history—what was later referred to by Fernando Bernardo in his book as "the Swaminathan years." Following this, the International Association for the Advancement of Women gave me their first International Prize for Service to Women. I am talking here not about the prize itself, but about 'leaving your footprints' on issues of importance. Gender is not just about getting a few women in here and there, but really impinging on the daily lives of large numbers of women.

The Gender Challenge in North Korea

North Korea was a challenge for me as the DG of IRRI. I could not get funds from anywhere to start work there. In 1985, Kim II-Sung invited me to visit—my predecessors could not go there as they were all Americans. North Korea was a clear case of feminisation of agriculture—all able-bodied men above 16 years were required to join the military. They had a one million strong army, which is not at all necessary for a small country like North Korea. They put me up in a seven star hotel in Pyongyang, a beautiful city with many hotels, an Arc of Triumph larger than that in Paris, and huge statues. But when you went out of Pyongyang, the conditions were miserable: no rural roads or markets and the women were full of complaints. How could they produce more, without any equipment or technical support? In fact, I had seen Russian tractors sinking in the paddy fields in Cambodia. They were too heavy and not designed for tropical countries. I met Kim Il Sung and said to him, "Mr. President, you have made women the custodians of food production. That's fine. They will do the job. But you will have to equip them. Provide them with facilities." The President of the Academy was with me. He said "The problem is we don't have the money." The only one who could help me was the United Nations Development Programme (UNDP) Resident Representative in Pyongyang, a Turkish man. When I told him the problems, he agreed to give $20,000: "That's all I have. You select 20 women. We can arrange a travelling workshop." They came to India, and the Government of India agreed to host them. So we had no problem concerning money. They visited the Bhopal Agriculture Engineering Institute, and when they left, I requested the government to gift them some implements. They were very happy. North Korea's recurrent food crisis is in part due to inadequate attention given towards addressing the needs of the women entrusted with the task of producing food.

IT as a Transformational Technology: The MSSRF Knowledge Villages

When working with the poorest and assetless, especially women, a question that always came to my mind was: what kind of asset can we give them to enhance their ability to earn? That is why I thought of new technologies: information technology (IT), biotechnology, etc. The first dialogue we organised in MS Swaminathan Research Foundation (MSSRF) on biotechnology led to the concept of 'bio-village'. Biotechnology doesn't only mean genetic modification, but also opens up possibilities for the production of bio-pesticides, bio-fertiliser, vermi-culture and other technologies. At that time, nobody had thought of using IT to help farmers. So we were far ahead in 1992 when we had a seminar on IT to discuss how what we called 'information villages' could be developed. I named them Village Knowledge Centres (VKCs), rather than information centres, as knowledge is interactive and two-way, while information is passive. In most places, women were trained to manage the VKCs. This programme, VKCs, has evolved into Village Resource Centres (VRCs), and today with satellite communication and mobile telephony it has become a truly transformational technology.

We recently had a meeting in some of the villages, where women said that IT has allowed them to come out of their homes: *'veetlarandhu veliyavanthutom'*—they felt liberated. Many people have come forward to support this initiative—International Development Research Centre (IDRC), the Tatas—we have been able to set up the Jamsetji Tata National Virtual Academy (NVA) with their help. The main idea behind the NVA is giving women self-esteem and recognising their contributions. As academicians, even without formal degrees, ordinary women have blossomed into extraordinary women.

While championing women's equal rights and entitlements over the years, especially in agriculture and the productive domain, MSS has come to recognise that women are constrained not just by lack of access to technology, skills and productive inputs, but equally by lack of time and the responsibility they carry, often unaided, for child care and reproductive work, which continue to remain unrecognised and unsupported. Sensitised to women's work burdens and drudgery in significant ways by Mina, from her early interventions in Delhi villages to later engagement with women's issues, he is now a strong advocate of support services for women, including childcare, and has come to see reproductive work as being almost inseparable from productive labour.

3

Education, Information and Social Mobilisation

Long before the RTI (Right to Information) and the RTE (Right to Education) became laws in 2005 and 2006, the important role of awareness, of making relevant information available to people, including children, and of mobilising them for socially relevant causes was clear to M.S. Swaminathan (MSS). When I decided to work with SEWA (Self Employed Women's Association), organising women bidi workers into cooperatives, while recognising the personal and practical difficulties I had to encounter, he and my mother were always very supportive. Three snippets from very different moments in his life demonstrate how goals can be achieved through taking people into confidence, whether children, farmers or local researchers and workers.

Mobilising School Children for Eradicating Filariasis

As a young child, in the 1930s, filariasis was endemic in Kumbakonam. Almost every third person suffered from filarial infection, locally called *Yaanaikkaal* or 'elephant legs'. I always wondered how this happened. My father, a renowned surgeon, a graduate from the Vienna School of Surgery, taught me that it was a man-made problem, not God given. Hence only men could solve it by their actions, not by praying to God. He wanted some authority, just to eradicate the filarial mosquito, so he stood for the municipal elections, and in 1934, was elected Chairman of the Kumbakonam Municipality. He believed in providing high quality medical care at no or moderate cost. This was his work ethic; he would not accept money from those who could not afford to pay. I was in school then, and one day we were all taken to the street by the teacher. We didn't know what was going to happen. We walked through the street with the teacher pointing out places in the street where mosquitoes were breeding. (In those days, there was no DDT, which came after World War in 1941-42.)

We were asked to either fill up the breeding grounds or spray them with crude oil emulsion. Within one year, the mosquitoes disappeared. We all enjoyed going around the street spraying crude oil on the mosquito breeding grounds. With a small amount of money, purely by education and social mobilisation, the filarial problem was solved. This taught me that we can achieve several things by education and social mobilisation, rather than in a technocratic way.

These days the government is buying fogging machines and spraying DDT, but the people are not involved at all. In fact, when I moved to Chennai in 1988, educated people didn't know that the malarial mosquito also breeds in clean water. They thought only slum-dwellers were responsible, rather than themselves. But the mosquitoes bred in their own overhead tanks and fresh water open wells! That is why my father emphasised on awareness, starting with school children. The values learnt in my childhood have always stayed with me, particularly the inspiration that even seemingly impossible tasks like the eradication of mosquitoes are achievable. I have followed these principles in developing my own programmes.

The ability to identify a problem, analyse its causes and find solutions, through critical and creative thinking, has been a hallmark of his life. One of his favourite terms, 'malady-remedy' analysis, draws its roots from medicine and his father, from whom he learned this lesson early in life.

Mobilising Farmers: National Demonstrations, Seed Villages and Krishi Darshan

While much has been written about the Wheat Revolution, popularly called the Green Revolution, the elements of information sharing through innovative communication strategies and social mobilisation are rarely discussed. As MSS notes, the yield revolution was only possible because the farmers were not merely conscientised, but could clearly see the benefits of the new technologies to themselves. Much before the debate on 'participatory development' began to be promoted by international agencies, he felt the need to engage with farmers in the villages, if a real difference was to be made. Working with the people and community empowerment were part of Gandhiji's philosophy, which he had internalised early on.

Once when we received the initial wheat genetic material from Norman Borlaug, a wheat breeder at the International Maize and Wheat Improvement Centre (CIMMYT), Mexico (awarded the Nobel Peace Prize in 1970), in September 1963, it was clear to me that with this material a yield breakthrough was possible. Every year PL480 wheat was being received under very humiliating circumstances. It normally takes around 10 years to develop a variety, have trials and spread the information through extension agents. I wanted to use this opportunity to 'purchase time', to leapfrog in terms of spreading the new varieties. I wrote to the Ministry of Agriculture that as farmers are the best judges of the value of scientific work, we should start a National Demonstration Programme in small farmers' fields, because anything demonstrated in rich farmers' fields would be attributed to affluence and not to technology. This was driven by my experience in 1958, where brigades of scientists went to the farmers' fields for three to four months to check the acceptability of a pest-resistant variety. The Ministry wanted to demonstrate in progressive farmer fields; these were rich farmers who would give them tea when they went there. My proposal was not approved.

Fortunately, in August 1964, C. Subramaniam (CS) became Agriculture Minister under Lal Bahadur Shastri's Prime Ministership. He had great faith in science. So he told Dr Pal, the then Director of Indian Agricultural Research Institute (IARI), that he wanted to meet his team of scientists; 15 or 20 of us met CS. He was very democratic, went from person to person. When he came to me, I mentioned that there was a great possibility of leapfrogging in production; I explained to him the potential of the dwarf wheat. I requested him to approve the National Demonstration programme in the fields of small and resource-poor farmers, rather than progressive farmers, to find out their reactions to the new seeds. Within two days the approval came. It cost only ₹ 500 per hectare and 1000 national demonstrations were organised. They were not only related to wheat but also to rice, jowar, bajra and other high-yielding varieties. That was a turning point.

The national demonstrations created a huge clamour for seeds. Jounti Seed Village was organised, where all the farmers took to seed production, and produced 3,000-4,000 tonnes of seeds from 800 hectares; 18,000 tonnes of seeds were also imported from Mexico to condense the time. We started in 1964 and by 1967-68, saw a major breakthrough, production rising to 17 million tonnes from 6 million at the time of Independence. From 1947 to 1964 wheat production rose to 12 million tonnes, mainly due to irrigation. During 1964-1968, we increased it by another 4 million tonnes. I took Indira Gandhi, the then Prime Minister, to Jounti Seed Village. But people were very pessimistic about our ability to overcome the 'PL480 syndrome'. To change defeatist attitudes, she agreed to my suggestion to release a postal stamp on the Wheat Revolution, and it was done in 1968.

Unfortunately CS got defeated in the 1967 elections, but the support given to pricing policy by Jagjivan Ram, the next Minister, was timely. Farmers will be enthusiastic about increasing yields only if they get decent prices for the surplus. Those three years, 1964-1967, were critical in terms of political support in whatever we wanted such as import of seeds and national demonstrations. Otherwise we would still have made the breakthrough, but it would have taken longer. So, the 1960s was a very exciting period. Many authorities referred to India as living from 'ship to mouth'. We were able to change that. It was amazing because people never thought it was possible.

Apart from demonstrations, it was important to share the information widely. In 1966, after Homi Bhabha's death in an air crash, Vikram Sarabhai succeeded him as Chairman of the Atomic Energy Commission. He was interested in the communication between scientists and the field, and wanted to use the space programme to facilitate this. Vikram and I went to many villages. He was excited by what he saw in the fields, and wanted to share this information with Indira Gandhi. In those days, it was not difficult to meet the Prime Minister, and he knew her very closely, as Ambalal Sarabhai's family was one of the leading industrial families to support the freedom struggle. So we went to her house. "We must start Krishi Darshan on TV. You have to inaugurate the programme," he told her. We were discussing this in the month of December, and Indira Gandhi gave the order to start Krishi Darshan immediately; she inaugurated it on the Republic Day. The bureaucrats came running to IARI the next day with a host of questions: How do we make the films? Where are the cameras? Where are the villagers? How to shoot? etc. Vikram Sarabhai was very generous and donated money for 200 TV sets from the Nehru Foundation. I asked the IARI Extension Division to take the cameramen to the villages, and help them shoot the films Krishi Darshan was inaugurated on 26 January. Thousands of farmers had gathered in her house, and she told them about the new opportunities. Krishi Darshan slowly grew in popularity and became a household word.

The next step was to make farmers enthusiastic about the increased yields. Two things were necessary: if the produce increases, there must be a market for it at a fairly decent price. That is why the Prices Commission and Food Corporation of India (FCI) were set up to purchase grain at reasonable prices. The decisions taken by CS and Jagjivan Ram were very helpful. Unfortunately, at the other end, post-harvest technology including storage and distribution had been neglected, and even in the present scenario. In my five-year programme for spreading dwarf wheats (1963-1968), I had suggested proper silos for storage. Morarji Desai called a meeting in IARI to discuss my note on storage, but the government did not do much. Farmers have two problems: seeds and markets. Both have to be solved, otherwise it becomes a grave issue, especially for small farmers.

Mobilising the Capacity of Locals: The Case of Afghanistan

Apart from children and farmers, he has been equally enthusiastic and willing to repose faith in local people—researchers, professionals and community members—even when, on the face of it, they seem to lack the capacity for the task at hand. Mobilisation to the cause and education appear as critical ingredients in achieving the goal.

The Ministry of External Affairs has recently set up a task force with me as Chair to oversee the implementation of agricultural projects in Myanmar and Afghanistan. A key proposal is the establishment of an Agricultural University of Afghanistan, on the model of Indian agricultural universities. By a decree, President Karzai has already transferred 1,137 ha of land with irrigation facilities in Tarnak Farm, Kandahar, for establishment of the proposed university, and the Governor of Kandahar has been appointed President of the university, which plans to have regional centres in the major agro-ecological zones of the country.

During discussions in Kabul in May 2013, President Karzai pointed out that assistance to establish this university will be the most meaningful contribution that India could make towards food and livelihood security of the people of Afghanistan, since nearly 80 per cent of the Afghan population depend on crop and animal husbandry, horticulture, forestry and agro-forestry and agri-business to make a living and nearly 60 per cent of the GDP (gross domestic product) comes from the farm sector. I felt we should start by establishing a Genetic Garden for Food and Livelihood Security, where a representative sample of the rich genetic diversity of Afghanistan could be cultivated and protected.

Rather than sending Indian scientists to Kandahar, given the security situation, I suggested that the best way forward would be to identify and nominate 25 Afghan scholars to undergo training in agricultural extension, agronomy, crop protection, horticulture and livestock management. IARI has already prepared an excellent training module for this capacity-building programme. The 25 selected scholars include both senior and junior scientists, men and women, and following the six months training, will form the faculty of the Agricultural University. The key here is to mobilise local capacities, and support local researchers and scientists, as this will make the intervention sustainable in the long run.

4

Upholding Human and National Dignity

While in government, MSS often reacted adversely to the state terminology, which referred to the poor as 'beneficiaries'. A deeply ingrained Gandhian value system made him emphasise the concepts of human dignity and recognition. This vision was clearly articulated in the plan for making Wardha District into Gandhi Zila during the Sixth Plan period. Yet good ideas can perish without political support. He could see early on the power of food self-sufficiency to enhance national dignity, giving the country considerable political clout globally. While the Emergency was a distressing period in modern India's history, he points to some of the positive contributions made by Indira Gandhi prior to this, and the differences between the two aspects of her political career.

Addressing the Needs of the Poorest: Antyodaya as the Basis for Sarvodaya

Indira Gandhi met Vinoba Bhave in Pavnar Ashram soon after she became Prime Minister again in 1980. He asked her to convert Wardha district to Gandhi Zila. I was in the Planning Commission then and was asked to chair a committee for this purpose, with Ramakrishna Bajaj, Devendra Gupta and Nandini Joshi as members. We worked hard developing the idea of Gandhi Zila. What is the definition of Gandhi Zila? It is easy to change the name, but the real idea was to eradicate poverty by enhancing the ability of the poor to earn their daily bread. Gandhi's idea was to enable the poor to feed themselves with human dignity rather than forcing them to beg. This was also my idea for the Food Security Bill; it needs to provide food with human dignity. At that time, 70,000 families were classified as BPL (below poverty line) in Wardha. Nandini Joshi developed a good programme with Khadi as an instrument to alleviate poverty; Bajaj helped in setting up small industries; Devendra came from *Magan Sangrahalaya* which had expertise in cottage industries. So we prepared a good plan; probably for the first time, there was thought on how to eradicate poverty completely from a district, not through doles or patronage, but by providing income and work security. The former perhaps satisfies our own conscience, but it doesn't respect the poor as thinking people.

Indira Gandhi liked it. Unfortunately, there was some conflict between S.B. Chavan, who became the Deputy Chairman of the Planning Commission at that time and Vasant Sathe, the Member of Parliament from Wardha. Without telling me, the file was transferred to the Maharashtra Government. As they did not want one of their senior IAS men in the Secretariat at Mumbai, they transferred him to Nagpur with the Gandhi Zila file. This was a punishment posting for him, so he asked me, "How do you expect me to develop a plan?" This political fight killed the plan. But I think it can be revived even now. Of course, it needs to be updated, but the principles were sound, as was the understanding of poverty and attention to human dignity. What the supporters of market reform today don't understand is that the market economy is more or less Darwinian, based on the principles of survival of the fittest. When you start with handicaps, how can you compete as equals? How can first generation learners, slum children, be compared with our children? We first need to equalise opportunities before free competition becomes a real possibility.

(Food) Self-sufficiency and National Dignity (Sovereignty)

One thing I that learnt during the 1960s and early 1970s was the importance of food self-sufficiency in enabling Indira Gandhi to take independent foreign policies so as to uphold national sovereignty. Food grains are indeed a political weapon. Abdul Kalam later said that Pokhran would not have been possible without the Green Revolution. While I do not support the nuclear bomb, food self-sufficiency helped us support the liberation of Bangladesh and feed the newly united Vietnam. People do not often see this relationship, but these historic decisions would not have been possible without food self-sufficiency.

By the early 1970s, the Americans were not happy with India due to the liberation of Bangladesh from Pakistan, as they were supposedly close friends of Pakistan. They stationed one of their warships near Calcutta, almost threatening us. Soon after came the Pokhran implosions in 1974, and sanctions were brought against India. But these became irrelevant since we had grains to feed ourselves, as well as more than a million refugees from Bangladesh. There was criticism that the camps were not good, and the food given was not nutritious. I was asked to go there. Of course in camps, there will be difficulties. But our government did the best it could in the circumstances.

But that was a drought year. Jagjivan Ram was the Agriculture Minister. Food stocks had come down and Indira Gandhi had started the Food for Work programme. We had to buy 2 or 3 million tonnes from the US on commercial terms. I went with Jagjivan Ram to meet the US Agriculture Secretary at the World Food Congress in Rome. He was rather rude. Jagjivan Ram told him very firmly, "I have come here not to beg, but to buy. I wanted to buy some wheat. If you don't want to give it, someone else will," and he walked away. My estimation of him really went up. Some of the old Gandhians had a lot of self-respect, which many of our leaders today lack.

Indira Gandhi has been criticised for the Emergency and many other things, but she had also taken some bold decisions prior to this. In 1974, the two Vietnams were united, and the Americans left South Vietnam. They urgently sent Madam Binh as a Special Representative of Prime Minister Pham Van Dong to meet Indira Gandhi. I was present at the meeting. She said, "We have no food. Lots of people will die of hunger unless India helps." Indira Gandhi knew we had just bought 2 million tonnes of wheat from America. She quietly asked the Food Ministry to divert the wheat to Vietnam. The Americans were furious, but could do nothing. The wheat was ours, we had bought it. Then she said to me, "Swaminathan you have to go there," and I did. When you flew over that country, you could see large orange-yellow patches. During the War, the infamous 'Agent Orange' was used and crops had been destroyed. The Minister in charge took me to Ho Chi Minh City (as Saigon had just been renamed) and we also visited the Mekong Delta.

In my report, I stated that the Mekong Delta, then with low yields, was a large untapped reservoir. North Vietnam had made some progress, but South Vietnam, because of uncertainties created by the war, was not able to develop food production. I suggested the setting up of a rice research institute in the Mekong Delta. The Prime Minister repeatedly told me how much India's support meant to them. In a reflex action I said, "Mr Prime Minister, in your dictionary the word impossible doesn't exist." He stood up, delighted, shook my hand and then spoke for an hour. That was the turning point. Once they knew how to handle the Delta, they were able to develop technology, their own varieties and public policies. Today Vietnam is a major exporter of rice, next only to Thailand. My student from IARI, Bui Bong, played an important role in this. He became Director of the Institute, and later Minister, because of his success in developing rice production technology appropriate to the Mekong Delta.

Westerners often criticise us for focusing on increasing food production to be food self-sufficient. They say that with resources, you can buy food anywhere. Yet food security is powerful; there is a larger dimension in terms of the role of agricultural advantage in global negotiations and national sovereignty, which critics of the technology, both national and others, fail to take into account. They never looked at the conditions we were living in. The rescue of Vietnam and Bangladesh and the Pokhran tests were possible only because of our food self-sufficiency. I wholly support the anti-nuclear movement and do feel that Pokhran should not have happened. But, right or wrong, the ability to perform those tests was facilitated by our independence in food requirements.

Farmers' Rights and the Right to Food

During colonial rule, Famine Commissions were appointed from time to time in order to address the problems created by recurrent famines. Between 1870 and 1900, nearly 30 million children, women and men died of hunger. A Famine Commission recommended the establishment of Departments of Agriculture by state governments, and the strengthening of agricultural research and education. In independent India, several commissions on agriculture have been set up from time to time; however, neither in colonial nor independent India has there been a commission for farmers. For the first time in

2004, the National Commission on Farmers (NCF) was set up by the Government of India, which I had the privilege to chair. We submitted five reports between 2004 and 2006 as well as a draft of "National Policy for Farmers". These reports have received strong support from most political parties, farmers' associations and scientific organisations. The National Policy for Farmers was also finalised and placed in the Parliament in October 2007.

To my sorrow, no action has been taken yet to implement the recommendations, particularly those dealing with farm women and men as human beings and citizens of the country and not just 'beneficiaries' of government programmes. What is urgently needed is an attitude change in those Bhavans dealing with agriculture so as to recognise farmers, men and women, as the custodians of our food security. International prices of food commodities are very volatile, so I always say that "the future belongs to nations with grains and not guns." The Food Security Bill, currently before Parliament, provides a legal right to food to 70 per cent of our population, but it can be implemented only with the help of the large number of farm families.

5

Motivating and Managing People

An important element of his attention to people has been putting in place systems and procedures to motivate people to do their best, and simultaneously providing opportunities to enhance their capacities and sense of fulfilment. Here, Mina's support and interventions have been significant.

Team-building at IARI

In the 1950s and 1960s, our research budget was very small and for every additional piece of work, one had to prepare a project and get it approved through a long procedure, which could take a couple of years to fructify. In the early 1960s, I was in a hurry and in every field, we wanted to purchase time. This was particularly true in relation to the multiplication of seeds of the new high-yielding, semi-dwarf wheat varieties. Since that Indian Agricultural Research Institute (IARI) had very limited land, we decided to work with farmers to produce the required seeds. The Jounti village in Delhi became the first Seed Village in the country. This work could be organised only with the help of research students. Led by the Student Union President, Dr Venkat Rao Gadwal, a large number of students willingly visited the village twice or thrice a week and worked with the farmers on the new agronomic practices needed for making the semi-dwarf varieties express their yield potential. This exposure to rural problems and realities had a life-changing impact on the students. Importantly, it created a sense of bonding not only between the students and rural families, but also with the staff and the research community at IARI. We all felt that we were working for a common purpose, irrespective of status.

Mina: I helped organise a group of staff volunteers to go to one of the nearby Delhi villages in the late 1960s, to explore what else the community, particularly the women, needed, apart from seeds and agricultural inputs. It was February. All the women, Jats and Dalits, left for the fields at 6 am and returned home by 11 am. The Social Welfare Board was running a *balwadi*, but the teacher came at 10 am, so it was no use to them. They challenged us to give them a *balwadi* that would run from 6-11 in the morning. This was indeed a challenge: how could we find a teacher who would reach the village that early in the morning? There were no buses running so early. We finally found the daughter-in-law of the village *Pradhan* (headman). The young woman was bright, interested and with high school education. She agreed to run the *balwadi* from 6-11 during the busy agricultural season from February to May. As we didn't have money, we provided some snacks and also taught her several games and activities. The village people happily collected some money to give her an honorarium. It was a small amount, but served as recognition of her contribution, that she was providing a useful service. After May, the work eased off in the fields and the timings could be relaxed. It was a year of great learning for all of us. My only regret is that I could not do anything for the children of the women agricultural labour working on the IARI fields.

Establishing the Agriculture Research Service: From Calamity to Opportunity

When I became Director General (DG) in 1972, the personnel policies of Indian Council of Agricultural Research (ICAR) were such that those who wanted a small increase in income, would have to change their jobs, unlike the Indian Administrative Service (IAS). Scientists were competing every month, jumping from post to post, just for a little more money. There was no continuity and much uncertainty. So I decided to develop an Agriculture Research Service (ARS) which would provide opportunities for professional growth and financial compensation, without changing one's post or line of work. Once in five years you get assessed on your work and can move to the next grade, without having to change your job. There were 400 scales when I joined, I reduced them to eight. A man or woman in

S1 can climb to S8 by assessment, I quoted the example of Borlaug. He was a Nobel Laureate but remained a wheat breeder. He did not have to become DG to get the compensation due to him. I proposed a scientist-centred system, delinking salaries from individual posts. (I myself was recruited as Assistant Cytogeneticist, and at retirement, was confirmed only as Cytogeneticist.) Getting this through however was not easy. Fortunately Jagjivan Ram and Indira Gandhi were supportive, while the Home Ministry was against such an all-India service. They emphasised that agriculture was a state subject, so it was not possible to set up a central service. I had stated that it was a service for the ICAR staff, not for the state governments.

Today, all ICAR scientists recognise the value of the ARS; it has proved to be a great blessing for agricultural research and has helped to enhance the self-esteem of scientists. These reforms were driven by the unfortunate case of suicide by a scientist who was well known to me. He felt aggrieved at not being selected for a higher post in the Division of Agronomy at IARI. All kinds of accusations were made. I was also a target as the head of the organisation, although I had nothing to do with the selection, as there had been a duly constituted Selection Committee of very eminent scientists. Nevertheless I felt there should be a proper enquiry into the points made by him in his last letter addressed to me. A very high level Enquiry Committee headed by a former Chief Justice of India (Justice P.B. Gajendragadkar) was set up. This committee found that the choice of the scientist selected for the position had been a fair and correct one, and the most fitting candidate had been chosen.

At our request, the Enquiry Committee also examined many aspects of the management of ICAR, including the selection procedures, which consequently led to the setting up of an Agricultural Scientists' Recruitment Board (ASRB) on the model of Union Public Service Commission (UPSC); setting up of the Department of Agricultural Research and Education (DARE) with governmental authority; and incorporation of changes in management practices, including adoption of the principle of rotation in the appointment of heads of departments.

Thus, a great human calamity which gave me intense grief was converted into an opportunity to address issues which led to the calamity. I have always believed that for every problem, there is a solution. In fact when I had established ARS, I visited all ICAR institutions for a malady-remedy analysis so that appropriate policy and procedural remedies for the maladies from which scientists were suffering could be found.

For in-service training for ARS recruits, I set up a staff college at Hyderabad, later renamed as the National Academy of Agricultural Research Management (NAARM). The training was in three parts. The first one, 'Know your country', was provided by specialised Planning Commission members on a vision for the country and problems of Indian agriculture. The next six months focused on 'Know your client, i.e., the farmer', and the final part was called 'Know your institution'. For many, this was a life-changing experience, as they had come with MScs or PhDs, but were neither aware of the larger vision and policy process nor the ground realities. At the other end, vice-chancellors of agricultural universities too were invited, and case studies of good and bad practices were discussed. I felt we should not have too many staff members of our own, so I called upon the expertise of existing training institutions like the Administrative Staff College in Hyderabad and the Indian Institute of Management (IIM), Ahmedabad. Unfortunately, there is a proposal now to convert NAARM into a deemed university—its in-service training character will then be lost. My hope has always been that NAARM would serve the same purpose in the field of agriculture as the National Defence College does in the field of defence.

IRRI: Building the Capacities of National Systems

In the first month in International Rice Research Institute (IRRI), I did a gap analysis to identify the rice-growing countries that did not have infrastructure for rice research, because my Indian experience had shown that only a strong national research system could take advantage of the advances made in international research. For example, when Borlaug sent material, we had the infrastructure and could use it, but Pakistan, though it had the same material, couldn't do anything with it. So the national research system is very important.

We must collaborate, not surrender. That is why I am sorry now that ICAR is handing over the national research system responsibility for important crops to international agencies.

In fact, I was asked by many countries, "Will you open an IRRI in our country?" I said "No, but I will help you start one of your own." The first one was the China National Rice Research Institute at Hangchow, where there is still a small plaque put up in Chinese, thanking me for setting up this institution. In China, I helped develop four rice institutes. The second was for hybrid rice at Changsha; a third for *azola* that is useful for biological nitrogen fixing, because when you get high yields, you also need to feed the plant appropriately. The fourth was the China National Gene Bank. Next was the whole of Indo-China—Lao, Cambodia, Vietnam—they are all rice-eating people, but there were no rice research institutes in the Mekong delta. They used primitive methods and got very low yields. In Vietnam, as I have already mentioned, India helped develop the infrastructure following the end of the war. I only supplemented this by training a large number of Vietnamese people at IRRI.

Cambodia was the last one—in fact, the contact was established through Mina. She had gone to Cambodia as part of her work with United Nations Educational Scientific and Cultural Organization (UNESCO). I had sent a letter through her to the Agriculture Minister, and they responded positively and sent me an invitation when she returned. When I visited in 1987, the country was in a bad condition. Due to Vietnamese presence, the Americans had asked all the allies not to help Cambodia monetarily. The only country I could get money from was Australia. Bob Hawke, the then Prime Minister, had come to Philippines to meet Cory Aquino when she became the President. I got 10 minutes with him to explain the programme. He agreed, but said it should be called the Indo-China programme. He gave one million dollars immediately. In fact, there is a beautiful book on the entire Cambodian programme written by an Australian, Don Puckridge. The Cambodian government was so grateful for my support in building their national agricultural research system that they gave me their *Sahametrei* award in 2006—the highest civilian honour for a foreigner.

When I was young, my mother used to tell me we were eating Burmese rice. In fact, a part of the Bengal famine was because when Japan occupied Burma, they stopped sending rice to areas controlled by the allies. I visited Myanmar, which was under military rule. The Agriculture Minister was General Yu Gong. He too asked me to set up an IRRI. I refused, but instead, we helped set up a National Rice Institute at Yezin. Canadians were the only ones to give money to Burma, and Dr Umali, Food and Agriculture Organization (FAO), Assistant Director-General (ADG) at that time, gave some money for training people at IRRI. This Institute is still doing well. I am now involved with strengthening this further with the rice biopark initiative of the Government of India.

In South Asia, the infrastructure existed; it was more a case of identifying gaps and building human resource capacity. Pakistan was very enthusiastic about developing its research capability in partnership with IRRI and we could hence make considerable progress in the development of new varieties there. My predecessor at IRRI, an American, had indicated that as an Indian I might find it difficult to work in China and Pakistan. It was the opposite—we had a very constructive and warm engagement in both places. For the inauguration of the Pakistan National Agricultural Research Institute, there were only three speakers. One was Zia-ul-Haq, the President; the American Ambassador as the Americans had funded it, and me. Even the Indian Ambassador was surprised and asked how I was invited. We had good relations with Bangladesh too under Sheikh Mujibur Rahman, both during the Martial Law period and later with an elected government, and also with Sri Lanka. In the latter, I helped mainly with human resource development. We enabled a number of professors from Jaffna University to get advanced training with financial support from Japan. We also provided them with some equipment to set up a Gene Bank. In these cases, it was only strengthening their capacity and adding more value. Unfortunately, India was not interested, the then Minister was negative and would not allow scientists to go abroad.

One thing that disturbed me was that while IRRI was based in Philippines, the country lacked its own national research capacity. When I went to the Philippines, people used to say that their rice tragedy was represented by the three Ts: typhoon (cyclone), *tungro* (viral disease) and Tanco (Secretary in charge of public policy). Tanco told me once, "You have a lot to do in developing appropriate varieties for us." I said, "The Philippines has over 8000 islands, and there are a lot of localised problems and variations, the varieties alone can't solve the issue." But he was not convinced.

On the day of the EDSA Revolution, my friend Dr Umali rang me up and said that *Radio Veritas*, a Catholic channel, was giving news of the revolution. They were calling for "people power" to stop Marcos' tanks. The nuns were blocking the tanks; as religious people, they could not be shot easily. Around 11.30 pm, some 50 boys and girls from the University of Los Banos came to meet me. The security rang me up. I knew it must be urgent, so I let them come. They had one simple demand. They wanted the buses from IRRI to go to Manila (the buses were meant for children of the international staff to go to the international school in Manila). I had to take a split-second decision. On the one hand, we were in Philippines, and Marcos was in power. On the other hand, I could see the students were agitated and wanted to go and help the freedom movement. I rang up the security and asked them to mobilise the drivers available to drop them in Manila and come back immediately.

This news reached Mrs Aquino. When the government changed, and I met her, she said "You helped our movement. What do you want me to do in return?" I asked her to visit IRRI. I showed her a blue print for Phil Rice that I had developed—the Rice Institute in Philippines. She asked me what the problem was in developing the institute. I told her about the lack of money. They immediately provided it with help from Japan and the Institute was set up. The first Director was a good man, who came from the same province as Marcos; yet when I recommended him as a suitable Director, she immediately approved his appointment. Conferring the Golden Heart Presidential Award on me on 10 November 1987, she cited my "untiring efforts in pursuing the establishment of a national rice research institute in the Philippines" as one of the reasons for the award.

To sum up, if we wish developing countries to progress in agriculture, we must help them to build strong National Agricultural

Research Systems (NARS). The stronger the NARS, greater is the benefit of the International Agricultural Research Centres (IARCs). Human resource development should receive high priority. These days there is greater worship of 'bricks' rather than brains. In my view, IARCs should not set up their own institutes in developing countries. Instead, they should help in the establishment of strong, multi-disciplinary national research institutes, as I did in the case of China, Myanmar, Vietnam, Cambodia, Philippines, and also Egypt, Madagascar and Tanzania. This will confer long-term benefits and also help strengthen the morale and capability of national scientists, working on national salaries.

Mina: One of the many reasons for MSS' immense popularity at IRRI and the confidence that the Filipino staff and students had in him was my usual 'social lubrication', but this time with a difference—it was more a case of breaking status 'ice' between staff paid in dollars and those in pesos. At the time, all the senior scientific positions, about 40 only, were held by 'international staff', while there were more than 1000 Filipino employees, men and women, at all levels. The residences of the two groups were also physically separate, a kind of social separation common in many international organisations.

I soon began relating to the Filipino community, from top to bottom. I started by learning the language, through private tuition, a language- learning programme on audio-tape, travelling to villages alone, making friends with people, and of course, watching boring TV shows because they were easy to understand! Soon I was fluent enough to take part in discussions, workshops and drama clubs, study Philippine traditional theatre, and could pass for a Filipina on the telephone. We began to invite Filipino staff home in Asian style—the whole family from eldest to youngest—and not just the husband-wife couple as in formal Western-style entertainment. And to serve them not only Indian food, but traditional Filipino food like roast sucking pig cooked for feasts, even giving them small portions of it to take home when they left, a Filipino custom that I had learnt, similar to the Indian habit of giving sweets or *tambulam* when guests depart. The staff was thrilled to feel at home in precincts of the expatriate 'compound', an enclosure where they had never before been allowed to set foot. The Union leaders became regular dinner guests, and there were no more labour troubles! MSS became President of the Staff Football Club, though he has never played the game, and I, of course, of the Staff Drama Club. There were students of almost all Asian nationalities at IRRI, and we used to attend all their national day celebrations. Since I spoke the language and travelled widely, I was familiar with the political situation, though no one at IRRI confided in me their close links with the 'insurgency' as it was called (until after Marcos was overthrown, when I realised that we had been living right in their midst, so to speak) and they must have guessed our sympathies were with the Revolution. That probably emboldened them to ask for the buses! By the time we left, MSS was wildly popular and worshipped like a hero, while I made my farewell speech in Tagalog to a thunderous applause.

Utilising existing expertise

I realised early on that there was immense expertise available; there were many people who were willing to make a contribution. My job was to facilitate this process. At MSSRF, we selected our trustees very carefully. We were very lucky to have V.L. Chopra, V.K. Ramachandran, Kissen Kanungo and Shyamsundar Nair as early trustees. They gave a lot of time for the Foundation. For example, Kissen took charge of the Wayanad land on behalf of the Foundation and Shyamsundar Nair provided guidance to the whole bio-village project. This is a key strategy in building an institution. Apart from a clear goal, which addresses a gap in research, it should be, in my view, a 'centre without walls'. This follows Gandhiji's concept of keeping 'your doors and windows open', and getting ideas from everywhere. As our salaries were low at that time, we tried to have a blend of young people who would be helped by senior people, like Kesavan, Balaravi, Velayutham, Arunachalam, John Joseph, Johnson, K.V. Raman, Sankaran, Rajagopal and many others. Many of them came as Guest Fellows, or accepted a small compensation and guided some of our key interventions. They had retired from government service and had pensions, but were still active. The institution started growing faster than what I had thought, so drawing on their expertise was invaluable.

6

Science in the Service of Society

One of his key and early understandings was that to be both effective and transformational, science is essential, but science alone is not enough. People have to come first; in his words, we need to put faces before figures. This ability to understand and work across levels and scales has been central to his approach. When I returned from having spent a summer in Uttarakhand, observing closely the appalling state of health services in the mountains, I wanted to train as a doctor. In our educational system, however, this was next to impossible, as I had not studied science for at least four years and was half-way through a history degree at Delhi University. Institute of Rural Management Anand (IRMA) had recently been set up and he encouraged me to think about other skills that I could offer in working constructively with rural people. The message was clear—concern and commitment should come before any technical skill to be of any use at all.

The farmer, the Scientist and the Policy-maker: The Green Revolution Experience

When I came to Indian Agricultural Research Institute (IARI) from Cuttack, Dr Pal was the Director. He was a breeder himself and recognised that something needed to be done to increase wheat yields. A quantum jump of 200-300 per cent was needed, 2-4 per cent would not do. While distinguished economists in the Planning Commission like V.K.R.V. Rao understood this point, they did not recognise what was happening in the farmers' fields. In 1965-66, Rao announced that he would be satisfied if India ever produced 15 million tonnes of wheat, but in fact we produced 17 million tonnes in 1967-68.

The Planning Commission was obstructive in getting 18,000 tonnes of seeds. However, with the import of the needed seeds from Mexico, through Borlaug, a small government programme became a mass movement. Only then could it be called a revolution. You don't have revolution with small and incremental steps. You have to unleash the farmers' enthusiasm. Their enormous enthusiasm spread like wildfire. Wherever you went, farmers were happy because for the first time they saw their produce doubled. A farmer who produced one tonne could now produce 2-3 tonnes. So the synergy between political will, scientific skill and farmers' own enthusiasm formed what I call the Green Revolution symphony. Farmers, politicians and scientists all played their part. Fortunately, C. Subramanian brought in a very fine Indian Civil Service (ICS) officer, B. Sivaraman, as Secretary, Agriculture (1964-1970). Sivaraman was willing to go round the fields with me, deriving his information not from files but from the fields, and was able to give a lot of support. The Minister could give orders, but the Secretary must be capable of following them through answering the questions, allocating resources, etc. People used to say that it was the good fortune of this country that it had the three SSSs: Subramanian, Sivaraman and Swaminathan. Each one played his part. So the lessons of this period were that science is a major trigger, but it must be rooted in the socio-economic reality of the farming world, along with policy support. Unless you relate science to what is possible with farmers in their own conditions, how will they accept it?

This was an exciting period. In the 1950s, we had started a lot of work on the fundamentals and genetics of wheat through the use of irradiation and other technologies, and developed excellent capacity, with many PhD students. People worked not only on wheat, but also on crops such as barley and rice. In 1964, C. Subramanian set up a panel of scientific advisors. K. Ramaiah, the first Director, Central Rice Research Institute (CRRI), Cuttack, was the Chairman and I was the Secretary. I gave a note in the second meeting, saying that we have made a yield breakthrough in five crops: wheat, rice, *jowar*, *bajra* and maize. As several were hybrids and seeds were needed to be developed every year, the High Yielding Varieties (HYV) programme was approved. Wheat and rice did well, but not the others. There were several reasons, but a major one was the market. Today maize price is high, but at that time, there was no market for hybrid maize. *Jowar* consumption was coming down with the Noon Meal Programme and

Public Distribution System (PDS) concentrating on wheat and rice. In the 1950s, when I used to visit Delhi and Punjab villages, *makki ki roti*, and *bajri ki roti*, were very popular; but their consumption has now declined.

In 1968, Indira Gandhi came to deliver the Convocation Address at IARI. C. Subramanian and Sivaraman came whenever we invited them. There was a strong relationship between science and public policy. Borlaug wanted to reproduce the same experience in Africa; he got the money, but the plans did not materialise. This was one of his biggest disappointments in life. I used to tell him that in India it was not merely science, but assured and remunerative markets and supportive policy that made the difference. Farmers could produce more, but this often resulted in further suffering due to the collapse of prices. Fortunately, in the 1960s, all links in the chain from production to consumption were pulled together in India. Today unfortunately this is no longer the case, responsibilities are fragmented—water is with one Ministry, land with another, and fertiliser and pesticides with yet another. There is no coherence in policy. It was the synergy between science and public policy in the 1960s that led to the spectacular progress.

Another thing I should mention here is the role of international collaboration. Borlaug's material saved us time; otherwise we would have had to extricate the genes for dwarfing from Vogel's material. Incidentally, Orville Vogel, a wheat breeder from Pullman, Washington State, was the first one to develop a dwarf variety outside Japan (Norin 10 is a short Japanese variety with a long panicle), but it was suitable for temperate, rather than warmer climates. We could still have done this, but it may have taken another three years. On our invitation, Borlaug visited India in 1963. We travelled across the Northern plains, and later he sent us a whole range of material from Pakistan, which was suitable to our conditions. We extracted some like *Kalyan Sona, Sonalika* and other amber grain varieties of soft wheat. In fact, we had such strong capacity, and Borlaug was so impressed, that he recruited many of them to the international research centres. I should particularly pay my tribute to the late V.S. Mathur, who developed outstanding semi-dwarf wheat varieties very speedily. I consider him among the greatest wheat breeders of the world. International collaboration becomes most fruitful when we ourselves know clearly what we want to achieve and have our own well-thought-out strategy for it.

This early experience has led to the adoption of a two-pronged strategy in all his later work, focusing on both ends—the farmer and the policy-maker. One example is the work on biodiversity in Kolli Hills, Eastern Ghats, which led to the formulation of the Plant Variety Protection and Farmers Rights Act in 1996, has been discussed later.

Link between knowledge and action

Very important is what I call bridging the Know-How Do-How gap—that between scientific knowledge and field-level action. There were at least three methods for bridging this gap that I developed—one was the *Krishi Vigyan Kendra* (KVK) next the land-to-lab and lab-to-land programmes, and third the creative use of agriculture students, especially in implementing drought management strategies. The KVKs involved high quality extension run by scientists, agricultural universities and non-governmental organisations (NGOs). A large number of them conducted lab-to-land demonstrations, but they emphasised on agricultural machinery to reduce drudgery. Once, a bullock-driven machine was brought for the demonstration along with a bullock from IARI. I asked, "Why have you not brought a farmer's bullock?" The person concerned said, "Farmers' bullocks are undernourished. They won't pull." These were the problems we faced in linking local reality with scientific advances.

Later, I started a Whole Village Operational Research Project. The first was at Sukhomajri. I employed P.R. Mishra from the Soil Conservation Institute, who later became known as the Himalayan Gandhi. In this system, what I later called Rural Systems Research, you take an area and look at the totality of natural resources. It is a project looking not at individual plots (half to one hectare in size), as in the national demonstration or lab-to-land programmes, but the whole watershed or the whole village. For example, if you want to promote ecological agriculture, then you need to understand the impediments in a holistic manner, because IPM (integrated pest management), for instance, can't be done by a single farmer; it has to be done on a group basis. That is why the Chinese are successful, as they can generate group work without our problems. The 'whole village' idea was not just about increasing crop productivity, but also addressing non-farm and off-farm employment opportunities. Sukhomajri was an ecological project in water harvesting, the motivation being the silting up of the Sukhna lake in Chandigarh. We wanted to contain this and regenerate the lake through water harvesting by the local people themselves.

This was one of my first Whole Village Operational Research Projects. Similar projects were then taken up elsewhere, especially in stabilising the desert areas of Rajasthan, where the Rajasthan Canal was getting silted up with sand from the desert dunes, which needed to be controlled. I also gave funds to Virendra Kumar, a scientist at Delhi College, to study the Alaknanda flash floods of 1971. He did a good study, and alongside people's mobilisation under the Chipko movement, this ultimately led to a 30-year moratorium on tree felling in the entire Alaknanda valley.

Making Law Responsive to People's Needs

From my days in Cuttack in 1954, I had a fascination for Koraput, because Koraput is what is called a secondary centre for the diversity of rice. In those days, over 3,000 varieties were cultivated in Koraput, now it has come down to 300. We started the biodiversity programme in 1994 in Koraput, and then further developed it in Kolli Hills, also in the Eastern Ghats and Kalpetta, Wayanad District, in the Western Ghats. This last one came about because we had a family plantation in Kalpetta, which my brothers were planning to sell. Instead of selling it and getting some money, we decided to give our share to the Foundation—first on a 10-year lease, and now permanently. Thanks to Madhav Gadgil, considerable amount of work has been done on the Western Ghats, but there was comparatively little available on the Eastern Ghats.

The biodiversity work has been conducted simultaneously at two levels: first at the grass-roots level to ensure livelihood security. For example, in Kolli Hills, the people now make a wide range of value-added products such as *ragi* malt. The other is at the level of public policy through legislation that recognises and protects farmers' rights. In 1996, I realised that the draft legislation I had prepared in 1994 didn't use the word Farmers' Rights in the title, but only spoke of Plant Variety Protection. So I renamed the second draft Plant Variety Protection and Farmers' Rights Act. Fortunately, Dr Sahib Singh, Chairman of the Parliamentary Committee on this legislation, visited MS Swaminathan Research Foundation (MSSRF), and I made a presentation on the rationale for this act. Some vested interests were trying to influence him not to include farmers' rights in this act, but I felt strongly that it was important to recognise the rights of the primary conservers and strengthen their livelihoods, and not just those of breeders, alongside biodiversity conservation. Both this and the Biodiversity Act, prepared in response to the Global Convention on Biodiversity (CBD), were first drafted in the Foundation, with Joint Secretaries from the Ministries of Environment and Forest and Law participating in order to ensure that the act was compatible with other legislation. One of the reasons for our success is that the knowledge is based on grass-roots realities rather than purely theoretical speculation.

7

Dealing with Criticism

There have been many times in his life when he has faced severe criticism of his work. The Green Revolution was seen as helping elite farmers rather than the poor, enhancing income and social inequalities in its wake. His systematic effort to collect rice germplasm from across the world to be held in Gene Banks was similarly criticised. It was not in his nature to be aggressive in his response, yet his personal integrity and confidence that what he was doing was for the 'larger good' and followed ethical principles, helped him find ways of dealing with such situations. My mother's support at these times became very critical. One of the lessons he drew from these challenging times was to set up systems of accountability, of checks and balances, to make sure that systemic misuse of power and knowledge become next to impossible.

The Green Revolution Critique

One of the criticisms of the Green Revolution was that it was not resource-neutral and benefited only rich farmers. Small farmers too can cultivate high yielding variety (HYV), but they lack the resources. Scale neutrality is not resource neutrality, and this is particularly severe for women farmers. They don't have Kisan Credit Cards (KCCs) and so are not able to easily access other inputs.

To overcome this problem of resource inequality, in fact, on our insistence, the Government started the small and marginal farmers' programme in 1968-69. Its main aim was to supply the credit needed to buy inputs, as without inputs there can be no output. If small farmers, who form a majority in India, were not involved, we could not have produced so much wheat—from 6 million in 1947 to 96 million tonnes in 2013. The only difference I would make is between farmers with water and without water. Water is needed to apply nutrients, to absorb any form of fertiliser or manure along with sunlight and convert it into output. Our un-irrigated areas have therefore remained disadvantaged. When I was at the Planning Commission, during the Sixth Plan, it was the only Plan where the agricultural growth rate at 5.7 per cent was higher than the general growth rate of 5.5 per cent, largely because of the allocation of over 12.5 per cent of the plan budget, the highest ever, to irrigation. If the allocations are correct, then there is no magic; we will see the returns in terms of equitable growth.

This is a problem I have also tried to grapple with in my later work. At MS Swaminathan Research Foundation (MSSRF), we have tried to address the needs of not only small and marginal farmers, but also the landless in our 'bio-villages' as mentioned earlier. Most of the projects work for not only improving agronomic and other practices with small and marginal farmers, but also equally developing non-farm and off-farm work for the landless.

Publication of False Data

In 1966, one of my PhD students, George Verghese, developed by mutation breeding a new wheat strain with amber seed, *Sharbati Sonora*, from the red seeded variety *Sonora* 64 received from Mexico. In 1967, with the help of the Rockefeller Foundation, we had bought some new equipment from the United States (US) to measure the amino acid profile of crop varieties. Since this was a complex instrument in those days, the Head of the Cereal Quality Laboratory (Dr A. Austin) was deputed to the company from where the amino acid analyser was purchased. On his return, he started analysing many varieties of wheat, maize and other crops for both their protein content and amino acid profile. During this work, Dr Austin found a higher lysine content in one sample of *Sharbati Sonora* as compared to its parent.

I was then the Director of Indian Agricultural Research Institute (IARI) and in popular lectures, I used to quote the findings of IARI scientists which might be of interest to the general public. At a gathering of vegetarians in 1967, I mentioned Dr Austin's findings. Later analysis revealed that the lysine content of both *Sonora 64* and *Sharbati Sonora* was more or less similar, although *Sharbati Sonora* had higher protein content. This experimental error was speedily corrected in the *IARI Research Bulletin* (No. 6, 1971); nevertheless I was accused of presenting false data on the lysine content in a wheat variety, an accusation that has since been repeated several times.

Science is the search for truth, hence I was very upset by these accusations. A detailed statement on the facts relating to this accusation was made in the Lok Sabha on 27 May 1976 by the Minister of State in the Ministry of Agriculture and Irrigation. The factual position was also published in the *Indian Journal of Genetics and Plant Breeding* (Vol.34(2), July 1974) and in *Science and Culture* (Vol.41: 43-47, February 1975). In the *Science and Culture* issue, Dr Austin had also described how this experimental error might have occurred in one case out of thousands of samples he had examined. Later, *The Statesman*, New Delhi, in its issue of 17 May 1977 repeated some of the allegations. In a reply to *The Statesman*, on the next day, I reiterated my faith in the scientific integrity of my colleagues, while also clarifying the difference between errors and falsification of data. With this statement, *The Statesman* closed the debate.

Despite these detractors, I was happy that several key people recognised my contributions and the steps I had been taking to improve the system. I was particularly moved by a letter from Shri Jayaprakash Narayan to the Prime Minister, Shri Morarji Desai, dated 14 October 1977, from Patna. In this letter, JP said:

> Dr M.S. Swaminathan, DG, ICAR, is a renowned scientist who has ably served the nation in the field of agricultural research. I have come to know that some people are mounting political pressure against him. Pained by this he intends to relinquish his office. It is unfortunate that politics should be brought into the field of scientific research. It will be in the nation's interest if Dr Swaminathan is allowed to continue his valuable work. I wish healthy traditions are established in the field of scientific research.

Equally important was peer recognition after careful examination of my work, leading to my election to some of the world's leading scientific academies such as the Fellowship of the Royal Society

(FRS), London, National Academy of Sciences, USA, and the Russian Academy during the period 1973-1977. I was also made a Founder Fellow of the Third World Academy of Sciences (TWAS). Nothing gives greater satisfaction to a scientist than when his peers rate his work as worthy of recognition. During the challenging times of the 1970s, my wife Mina stood by me as a tower of strength. Without her support, I would not have been able to convert calamities into opportunities for progress. Another person to whom I owe much is the late Dr K. Kanungo, a friend, philosopher and guide during the trying times I went through. So clearly, one should not be afraid to face difficult periods in life. What is important is to follow Shakespeare's dictum: 'To thine own self be true, thou canst not then be false to any other man.'

'The Gene Robbery' Debate

I am a geneticist, but this has always been an area that has evoked some criticism and controversy, including, at present, around 'genetically modified crops'. Much of this is due to lack of information and understanding on one hand, and lack of transparency by research organisations on the other. An important priority for me as DG, IRRI, was to strengthen long-term services like maintaining the Gene Bank, as the loss of every gene limits our options for the future. When we first started the programme in Cambodia, mines had destroyed many of their varieties; we could reintroduce the original Cambodian varieties only because they were held in the IRRI Gene Bank. Today there are over 110,000 varieties of rice, out of a total of around 1,50,000 in the world, available in the Gene Bank at IRRI.

The Gene Bank often aroused ill-informed criticism and talk of bio-piracy. An accusation that I helped IRRI to get hold of valuable Indian germplasm in rice for conservation in their Gene Bank was made in an article in the *Illustrated Weekly of India* on 23 March 1986.[1] The same journal had earlier carried an article by the same author titled, "The White Revolution: A White Lie" attacking Dr V. Kurien and

1. This journal ceased publication many years ago.

the Amul Dairy Cooperative. Scientific exchange of germplasm was referred to as gene robbery. Although I was personally named in the attack, the article referred to earlier events when I had no connection with either IRRI or ICAR management. My detailed reply, point by point, was published by the *Illustrated Weekly of India* with a comment that they were closing the debate with my reply.

My philosophy has been one of transparency. Once at IRRI too, an Australian journalist came to write against the Gene Bank. I gave her all the facts, and said to her, "If you have a doubt, please ask. If you are still not satisfied, you can criticise us, but please don't make ill-informed comments." She became an enthusiastic supporter by the time she left. Apart from that, I also wanted to establish systems of accountability. Hence, I placed the International Rice Collection under the supervision of an International Rice Board, even though it was a part of IRRI. Apart from Cambodia, native varieties have also been provided to Rwanda and Burma from the Gene Bank.

I was also encouraged by the international recognition of my work on collection, conservation and sustainable use of crop genetic resources. I was elected as President of the World Conservation Union (International Union for Conservation of Nature; IUCN) and also as Independent Chairman of the Food and Agriculture Organization (FAO) Council, which established, at my instance, a Commission for Plant Genetic Resources. I also served as Chairman of the Keystone Dialogue on Plant Genetic Resources, which helped to resolve several issues relating to exchange of germplasm. This public confidence in my integrity and dedication to the cause of biodiversity conservation and equitable sharing of benefits has given me the strength to continue promoting international cooperation in genetic resources conservation and utilisation.

Mina: Both these accusations disturbed him deeply at the time. On the gene robbery issue, he had the facts for the rebuttal, but seemed unable to put them together in a convincing way. I took all the material from him, shut myself up and rewrote it, using the two column table he has mentioned and writing up the rest in a more journalistic style suited to the publication. He signed it, and it was published. I think he was able to overcome the pain, because he knew that though some things had gone wrong, he had not contributed to wrongdoing in any way.

8

Dealing with the State

Issues of Governance

During the 1979-80 period, when MSS (M.S. Swaminathan) held the position of Principal Secretary, Ministry of Agriculture, an administrative rather than research position, he confronted financial and moral corruption at close quarters. These too were stressful years; yet he found ways of dealing effectively with the situations in his usual upright style, upholding principles of transparency and public accountability. The lesson, as he says, is to "keep the interests of the country as the bottom-line"; officers should not be afraid to speak up against authority in the interests of the country. One should identify with causes rather than individuals for the success of institutional mandates—in this case, a hunger-free India and conservation of biodiversity, rather than personal gains.

The Drought of 1979: Dealing with Bureaucratic Opposition

In July 1979, an interim government took charge under the leadership of Charan Singh. Unfortunately this was a drought year. The Agriculture Ministry was at that time responsible for dealing with all natural disasters. I knew that this was an interim government, and if something went wrong because of the drought, they would blame me too. So I went to Charan Singh and said, "I need political support. Please set up a Cabinet Committee headed by Yashwant Rao Chavan (a respected Congress leader) who has vast experience in handling drought in Maharashtra." This was done and proved prudent. As soon as we came to know that there was severe drought, I asked for two million tonnes of wheat for an open-ended Food for Work programme. The Planning Commission wrote two pages against this project. I gave a note on the consequences of cutting the budget and asked the Secretary, Planning Commission, to include it in the minutes. He asked me why I was getting annoyed. I said I was not annoyed, but simply asking him to include my note in the minutes. One has to deal with them, each one according to his/her personality.

Since I was the Secretary, I collected the comments and sent the proposal to the Cabinet Secretary, who asked the Prime Minister for advice in the face of many adverse comments. In this case, fortunately, Chavan immediately called a meeting on the proposal I had sent, heard the opposition from the Planning Commission and Finance Commission, but finally managed to get the sanction for the two million tonnes of wheat. But they refused to sanction any additional staff. Then I spoke to the Vice Chancellors of the agricultural universities for help, and we mobilised agricultural students across the country to aid this effort. A journalist from London, the daughter of the then British High Commissioner John Thompson, wrote an article entitled 'The Famine' that might have been in *The Economist* of September 1979. She described how the drought was handled. I had a detailed drought management system; terminology like 'crop weather watch group', still in use, was coined by me.

The message is that if you have a clear idea of what you want, or what needs to be done, it makes sense to get support from politicians and also build bridges amongst other stakeholders. Jyotirmoy Basu, a Communist MP from Diamond Harbour and a strong critic of mine, wrote me a nice letter when I became Agriculture Secretary, saying "We have often disagreed. But one thing I like about you is that you function on the basis of agree to disagree." In a democratic system, unless you carry the political system with you, you can't get support.

Dealing with Financial Corruption

The Charan Singh government had only six months in office; the elections had been announced for December 1979. The then Agriculture Minister came from the co-operative movement, but somehow seemed to be under pressure to make money in these six months. I received a file one day on the export of 25 crores worth of ivory from Rajasthan. This ivory consisted apparently of bangles and necklaces worn by poor women. But in 1972, the Indira Gandhi government had banned the export of ivory to prevent poaching, so I wrote this on the file. I had a suspicion that the Minister or someone close to him had been bribed. He then sent for Nalini Jayal, the Joint Secretary, and tried to convince him saying they were poor widows and needed the money. Then I said, "I have only written on the file, he can overrule me." Jayal was a conservationist and supported what I had written, but the Minister used to call him directly. Once the Minister said to me, "Swaminathan, there is a very big drought, and you are busy managing it. So don't misunderstand if I call your Joint Secretary directly I want to relieve you of this burden." I called all my officers and told them, "This is an interim government. If the Minister asks you to do something wrong, don't do it. Papers with potential for problems should go through me, and not directly to the Minister." Later they thanked me, saying "We could have been in serious trouble."

The Minister then complained to Charan Singh saying the Secretary was against the welfare of poor widows who wanted to sell their bangles, and was holding up the file. I got a call from the Prime Minister. I told him, "Sir, this is very dangerous. Ivory export has been banned and this is a proposal to sell 20-25 crores worth of ivory." So he asked what we could do. I suggested setting up a small investigation to find out where the ivory stocks came from. He asked who would investigate. I proposed three people and he signed it. The Minister was waiting anxiously to know the result of our meeting. When he heard that an Enquiry Committee had been set up, he was shocked, and no more was said about the matter.

In another case, $250 million worth of fishing boats were to be purchased from the Japanese. Two companies were in competition, and again I suspected possible bribery of not one, but two ministers. Unfortunately, they had invited me to a meeting to discuss this, where they were openly fighting with each other, accusing each other of taking money. I took it to Charan Singh and asked him to set up a committee headed by a Vice Admiral or someone of that rank in the Navy. He said, "Give it to me in writing I will sign." He did, and the case was closed. But my respect for Charan Singh went up. The man himself had no stake in this.

Dealing with Political Differences

Another big problem I faced was with the Silent Valley project. The Agriculture Ministry was in charge of forests at that time, the Ministry of Environment was set up later. There was a large electricity project of 200-300 MW power coming up in the Silent Valley. I went there with the Inspector General (IG) of Forests and wrote a report on it. The purpose for which the forest was being cut down was twofold: water and power. I got information on ground water from the Coimbatore Central Groundwater Board. There was more water than needed. Also, the Idukki area was fortunately able to generate additional power. My report set out ways to meet the water and power requirements without sacrificing the Silent Valley Forest.

When I went to Charan Singh, he said that the Silent Valley project was approved by the previous Morarji Desai government, so he could not reverse it. When Indira Gandhi retured to power in 1980, her supporter asked her to visit several temples across the country to restore a sense of both faith and optimism. One of the temples she visited was Guruvayur in Kerala. She said she wanted to read my report on the plane and take it up with Karunakaran, a prominent Kerala Congressman. After reading the report, she decided that the project must be stopped. She called a meeting with the then Chief Minister of Kerala, Nayanar, of the CPI(M). He brought his own set of scientists who were in favour of the project. After an hour's discussion, no agreement was reached and Indira Gandhi had to leave. She asked me to chair the rest of the meeting. We agreed to set up a committee headed by M.G.K. Menon, an eminent scientist, who came from that region. Menon did a detailed study which took some time, and I had left for the Philippines by then; but finally his report noted that the Silent Valley was an ecological treasure that could not be sacrificed at any cost.

In the meantime, Karunakaran became the Chief Minister in 1982, the Silent Valley Biosphere Reserve I had recommended was set up, and alternate arrangements for water and power for the region negotiated. That was my last act before going to the Planning Commission—saving the Silent Valley with the help of Indira Gandhi.

Experiencing Democracy First Hand

I served as a Nominated Member of the Rajya Sabha from 2007-2013, an experience which helped me understand the strengths and weaknesses of our Parliamentary Democracy. One of the highlights of my tenure was the opportunity to vote in favour of the Bill in order to reserve one-third of the seats in the Parliament for women (Constitution [Ninety Sixth Amendment] Act 2010). The socio-political empowerment of women, I believe, which started at the *panchayat* level, needs to be extended up to the highest decision-making bodies of our country so as to hasten the end of all forms of gender inequality and injustice.

While the issue-based support extended by all parties to important pieces of legislation gave me happiness, I feel sorry that my Private Member's Bill entitled 'The Women Farmers Entitlements Bill, 2011' could not come up for discussion before the end of my term. On two occasions it was listed for discussion, but unfortunately on both the occasions, the proceedings were disrupted, leading to adjournment of the House. I hoped that soon a consensus will emerge among leaders of political parties that both the Question Hour and the time allotted to Private Members' business should be out of bounds for disruption. In the latest Gender Inequality Index by United Nations Development Programme (UNDP), we occupy the 132nd position among 148 countries. This is a sad situation and without attention to the problems of rural women and women farmers who constitute the majority of women in our country, neither livelihood and food security, nor gender equity can be achieved.

In my farewell speech at the Rajya Sabha, I said (please see Annex 1 for the full text of the speech):

> As a biologist, I wish to cite an outstanding example of democracy at the household level. Charles Darwin is well-known for his path-breaking work in elucidating the origin of species, including ourselves, through evolution. Darwin's wife, Emma, was a staunch Catholic and the theory of evolution was considered blasphemy by Catholics and several other religious groups at that time. She was once asked how she managed to

live peacefully with Charles, considering that his theory of evolution was unacceptable to her. She replied that Charles lives by reason and she by faith. What leads to faith is feeling and not reasoning; so they agreed to disagree and lived happily together.

This represents the very essence of democracy for me.

9

Contextual Embeddedness and Cultural Diversity

Contextual awareness is a key principle of anthropology and the social sciences, but a rare sensitivity for a scientist. Perhaps the very nature of agriculture, and the differences in productivity based on different soil types and weather conditions, technologies and divisions of work, gave him the strong conviction that modern science cannot achieve change on its own, but needs to blend with the local cultural context. His belief that livelihood security of the poor has to go hand in hand with ecological security has informed programmes at MS Swaminathan Research Foundation (MSSRF), but with fast changing contexts, driven by many external factors—education, markets, technologies and changing aspirations—he also recognised that needs change; hence programmes need to be reviewed periodically to check their continued relevance on the ground institutions because they tend to become complacent as they mature and get known. Is there still a niche for the work, or is it merely routine, is a question always at the top of his mind.

MSSRF Building: Harnessing the Sun and Rain Water

Tamil Nadu is in a rain shadow region. Water for both domestic and agricultural use is in short supply, and the aquifers near the coast are being over-exploited. But we have an abundance of sunlight. So when we designed our building in Chennai, our architect Venkat was asked to incorporate methods of harvesting both rain and sun. The building is designed to harvest rain water and store it above or below ground. Likewise, the use of electricity for lighting rooms has been minimised by the use of natural light to the farthest extent possible. In addition, a solar photovoltaic system was set up which provides uninterrupted power supply to all computers. One of the objectives of this was to showcase the possibilities of such simple actions, especially for other institutions and for farmers and rural people who often visited us.

Finding an Institutional Niche through Consultation

A key principle underlying the setting up of MSSRF has been the effort to fill critical gaps in knowledge and practice. In my mind, I was clear that there was no point in setting up one more centre, because there are hundreds of research centres in India. The research has to be both anticipatory—anticipating farmers' problems—and participatory—finding collective solutions. I hence wanted land for a building, but not to develop our own farms, as I believed that we should work with farmers in their own fields. By the end of 1989, we had land in Taramani, given by the then Government of Tamil Nadu under Karunanidhi's leadership.

But before the building could be designed and built, we needed a place to start work. Indian Institute of Technology (IIT) Madras invited me to be a Visiting Professor; they gave me two rooms, and this is where I met Rajeshwari and Raman. They had a project on sea grass beds in the Gulf of Mannar area. India has a vast coastline, but the sea and land interface has never been looked at in an integrated way. The Fisheries Institute and Department were looking to capture and culture fisheries, but not at coastal agro-forestry, or mangroves, which are good breeding grounds for fish. We organised a small dialogue in IIT, with 15-20 people, on the concept and design of a coastal systems research project.

Around this time, I had gone to Japan to deliver a lecture at the Climate Conference, chaired by Dr Saburo Okita, Foreign Minister of Japan, who had received the Magsaysay Award along with me in 1971. At the end of the lecture, he seemed enthusiastic about the idea of anticipatory research to develop material for salt tolerance, sea water tolerance, mangrove conservation and so on, and recommended to the Japanese government to support such work. Unexpected support also came from a Japanese industrialist, who after listening to my lecture invited me for breakfast and gave a cheque of US$ 100,000 for our mangrove work. This helped leverage support from the Department of Biotechnology to establish a genetic garden of mangroves at Pichavaram. Apart from financing us through the International Tropical Timber Organisation (ITTO), the Japanese also asked me to chair the setting up of an International Society for Mangrove Ecosystems (ISME) at Okinawa, which is very rich in mangroves. From earlier experiences of working on rice, wheat and potato, this was a clean break for me—something new and refreshing, and clearly contributing towards filling a knowledge gap. No one else in the country was working on this issue.

Mina: At about this time, I had made friends with a Kattaikoothu artist (a traditional theatre form of northern Tamil Nadu) and became an impassioned student of the form, travelling to remote villages to see performances. My friend Rajagopal had got a small grant from the Ministry of Environment to develop a performance to create awareness on the theme of ecological sustainability, and I collaborated with him. I developed the story, while he developed the text, music and dances, rehearsed the play with his groups, both adults and children, and performed it. We used the traditional concept of *Pancha Bhootham*, or Five Spirits, representing the five elements—water, fire, earth, air and space—and how they rebel as a result of Man's ill-treatment, leave earth and withdraw to heaven. They can only be persuaded to come back if a crore of trees, or a forest, is raised in one night. A young couple takes up the task, and with the help of a bull who ploughs, a parrot who drops the seeds, an elephant who waters the field, and a dog who guards the seedlings all night (all the animals representing various Hindu gods), the forest miraculously rises up by dawn. This play has been sponsored by the Forest Department for countless performances in villages, schools and colleges, and a video has also been produced so that scientists and NGOs can use it where the drama group cannot reach. This was my 'value-addition' to the mangrove forest restoration programme!

Drawing on the Military in Contexts of Conflict: A Lesson from Burma

Burma, now Myanmar, has a lot of germplasm, similar to what we have in our North-East. However, this was not collected because these were very disturbed areas. When I went to Myanmar from International Rice Research Institute (IRRI), I told General Yu Gong that he should give some protection to our collectors. The General said: "Why Swaminathan, why do you want to send your people? You train my soldiers on how to collect and what to collect, and they will do this for you." We made a very good programme; I was there for the first two days. T.T. Chang ran the programme, explaining to the generals and the soldiers how to collect what we call 'passport data' about the plant. They collected about 9,000 varieties. I must give credit to General Yu Gong for opening my eyes to this potential.

Many disturbed areas are very rich in biodiversity. It is not always possible to send scientists there, as we cannot expose them to risks. I remember in the 1960s, when we started the Assam Rice Collection, there was a lot of disturbance in the North-East, including in Nagaland. I stayed myself at Makokchung, in the midst of the forest, occupied by the Aos who engaged in slash and burn cultivation. I didn't want to expose my scientists; rather I wanted to give them confidence by staying with them. We have a collection of 7,000-8,000 varieties from there. I had met the General before going there, but at that time I never thought of using the army people. In fact, they were disliked and the General advised me to go into the forest without them—that way we would be safer. Now things are worse; war and weapons are much more sophisticated and ruthless. What is important, I think, was the use of creative strategies to initiate a systematic process of collecting varieties not just from established areas, but also 'hotspots' that are often disturbed. This helped us almost double the collection in the Gene Bank.

10

Maintaining High Ethical Standards

This is perhaps the most critical of all the principles, encompassing both scientific and intellectual ethics, displaying fairness and fair-play in credit-sharing and authorship arrangements, as well as financial integrity. Professional, financial and intellectual integrity form the bottom line.

Only through strict adherence, can not only just and lasting relationships be built between both colleagues and collaborators, but meaningful constructive work can also be undertaken. This was a principle strongly ingrained also by Dr V. Kurien, whom I often got a chance to hear while at Institute of Rural Management Anand (IRMA), and whose impeccable personal integrity and zero tolerance for any transgression—personal or financial—contributed to his success. Strong ethics can make a person unpopular, draw criticism, yet in the interests of the larger cause and for long-term sustainability, some sacrifices often become inevitable.

Challenges Confronting a Research Organisation

A fundamental need for any good organisation, particularly one concerned with the development of new knowledge and technologies for the benefit of people, is a strong ethical foundation. In a scientific institution, ethical commitment has different dimensions. One is a purely scientific dimension, related to credit sharing. In fact, when we started the MS Swaminathan Research Foundation (MSSRF), I circulated a note saying honorary authorship should be completely prohibited, but credit should be given where it is due. Leaders have to set the example in this respect, not let a student or research assistant feel obliged to add the leader's name as author. While these power relations remain and need to be negotiated all the time, I think today students and younger people are also becoming bolder and more aware, and are able to talk openly to their professors. Also many journals, including *Science*, now require the authors to certify that there are no honorary authors. So I do think the awareness of ethics is spreading, yet we cannot take it for granted.

It is for this reason and the desire to share credit that I have always avoided using awards for my personal needs or projects. Even if the idea has been mine, in an applied field, putting it into practice has required support from many research scholars. So while recognition of an individual is important, it is also necessary to acknowledge that this success is owed to a number of other people. That is what I have always thought, and hence whether it was the World Food Prize or the Honda Prize, each one of them has gone towards a common purpose, rather than for personal use. A second part of scientific ethics is plagiarism; several people now use the Internet to plagiarise. We had a few cases of plagiarism at MSSRF, and the guilty parties were immediately dismissed. Scientific research is for truth, and scientific ethics, therefore, involves a very strong moral character.

At the International Rice Research Institute (IRRI), while there was no Ethics Committee, people by and large demonstrated ethical behaviour. There was only one problem area, and that was credit-sharing, especially with the local staff and with national research systems. In India, even today, some people think that the science behind Green Revolution began only with wheat. As I have explained in my article on the Yield Revolution (2013), this was not the case; in fact, the seeds of Green Revolution were sown in 1949 in the fields of the Central Rice Research Institute (CRRI), Cuttack, by K. Ramaiah and his colleagues, with a breeding programme designed to impart responsiveness to fertilisers by crossing *japonica* and *indica* varieties. When scientists are well known and work at the international level, there is a tendency to take the credit for themselves. I often told the scientists at IRRI, whom I nominated for prizes:

> I am nominating you because you are the Head of the Department, but your work has been shared by many others. You have been drawing an international salary for your whole life, so at least you can share your award with those who contributed to these successes.

A second aspect of ethics, especially for those in managerial positions, relates to financial integrity. Funds, particularly to a foundation like MSSRF, come from different sources and with well-defined objectives. Hence, the money has to be used for the particular work for which it was obtained and not diverted to other purposes. So, financial integrity comes into play in two ways. First, making sure that money is used for the decided purpose and second, ensuring that no money is misappropriated.

Finally, it is important that staff have a feeling that lack of integrity will not be tolerated. If the bottom line of the personnel and administrative policies should be a firm commitment to professional, financial and intellectual integrity, only then that institution will be able to harbour lasting friendship amongst colleagues. I have seen colleagues fall out on the sharing of credit, parting ways when they feel that their contributions have not been appropriately recognised. So in MSSRF, we have tried to promote a culture of honesty, of ethics and of financial integrity. Fortunately, in the first 10 years, high standards were set. But this can be very fragile, if it is not nurtured and reinforced. Exceptions may prove the rule, or undermine it. For example, if you know somebody has completely plagiarised and condone it, others may follow suit; the same goes for financial misappropriation or sexual misdemeanour. So there must be a firm message, whenever there is a transgression of these fundamental ethical principles.

We are therefore now institutionalising the principles of ethics and have set up an ethics committee under the Board of Trustees. We already have some codes of conduct, such as the Gender Code, but the ethics committee is now tasked with clarifying guidelines on a range of issues—whether personal behaviour, professional ethics or financial dealings. With growth of an organisation, there needs to be a well-defined and transparent ethics policy, which people should understand.

Mina: Having worked in several institutions at practical levels, by now I had enough institutional and managerial experience to contribute in that area, in addition to managing my own projects in child education, drama and gender. I began by introducing various activities for social mixing of the staff at different levels, like sports, picnics and exposure visits (including the ecological play), but their social and managerial value was not appreciated by the management and they were dropped after a few years. At first, the only interaction among staff was the formal scientific weekly seminar in Chennai, and the Annual Conference, which was also a series of scientific presentations with hardly any time for discussion. But I did succeed slowly in promoting regular exchange and interaction at various levels—horizontal and vertical, within and between disciplines, programme areas and field sites—through a number of planned theme based workshops, inter-disciplinary discussions, inter-site meetings, and other non-hierarchical strategies, as well as staff participation in management. One of the results of the latter was a flexible system of support services for women staff working in rural areas. Another was the development of a system of annual staff evaluation as a participatory exercise, led by a well-known specialist in human resource management. Finally, as a Trustee and Chair of the Personnel Committee of the Trustees, I led the development of a Personnel Policy, and also developed a Gender Code, both with organised feedback from the staff. Some of these developments have come to stay, others have not, but that is natural in any developing institution.

Government Procedures: The Civil Services Code of Conduct

In my earlier career in the government, we were subject to the Government's Civil Service Code of Conduct which provides an extensive set of rules and expectations around financial integrity, personal behaviour, etc. There was also an annual Confidential Review (CR), which recorded any doubtful or unfavourable characteristics of the person. These CRs are examined during the promotion process; if you have worked beyond the efficiency bar for five years, you will be promoted, but if you have a few black marks, you can also be dismissed. So there were rules, and these rules were quite transparent. I think this is something we need to learn too—rules and procedures need to be clear and transparent, if we are to facilitate work that requires high levels of commitment. Ad hoc decisions, criteria for which are not clear, will only create discontent and de-motivate people from putting in their best.

11

Unfinished Agendas

M.S. Swaminathan (MSS) has worked non-stop in the interests of India's agriculture, and more importantly, its farming men and women, over the past six decades. I started this project seeking to answer the question of what keeps him going; so at the end of our conversations, given the mass of information on his achivements, I asked if he still had any unfinished dreams. Unsurprisingly, he set out a huge agenda—that of addressing the Indian enigma of a high malnutrition burden in the midst of adequate grain availability.

From my childhood, I have observed, both in Thanjavur District of Tamil Nadu and Kuttanad in Kerala, the widespread prevalence of anaemia in children and mothers in rural areas. Both these districts are granaries of their respective states. Why then such a high incidence of malnutrition? This has always bothered me. It is not just calorie intake, but clean drinking water and sanitation that constitute the basic requisites for a healthy life. Protein hunger and hidden hunger caused by the deficiency of micro-nutrients like Vitamin A, Vitamin B12, iron, zinc and iodine are also debilitating. We need a holistic approach to eradicate the problem of malnutrition, with concurrent attention to calorie deprivation, protein hunger and hidden hunger.

My frequent visits to villages in Delhi, Punjab and other parts of North India from the mid-1950s also made it clear that eliminating the malnutrition burden is a priority task for those working in the area of enhancing agricultural production. Evidence started coming in from the 1960s about the potential adverse effects of maternal and foetal under-nutrition on the cognitive abilities of a child in latter years. This led to my presenting a talk on the threat of intellectual dwarfism in the mid-1960s at a Vegetarian Congress, where I emphasised that we should provide horticultural remedies, both through selection from nature and by breeding, for major nutritional maladies. A food rather than a drug-based approach would be both effective and economical.

I am convinced that an innovative science-based marriage of nutrition and agriculture can make a significant contribution in this area. When I became the Director General (DG) of Indian Council for Agricultural Research (ICAR) in 1972, one of my early steps was to create a position of Assistant Director General, Nutrition, in ICAR. We introduced a course on nutrition in the syllabus of the agricultural and veterinary colleges in order to familiarise students with the opportunities available to overcome malnutrition through agricultural and animal husbandry pathways. Unfortunately, the curricula have not developed further to explore new opportunities for mainstreaming the nutritional dimension in farming systems research.

So I have now designed a Farming Systems for Nutrition (FSN) methodology. FSN will provide a mechanism for ensuring that small farm families, who constitute a considerable proportion of the malnourished, will be able to overcome the major nutrient deficiencies in their diet. Fortunately, we have received some funding for such work from the Department for International Development (DFID), UK, and I am quite excited about the possibility of making a major dent—not only on maternal and infant malnutrition, but also on malnutrition in general among the rural population. Now that the National Food Security Bill will help us overcome poverty-induced calorie deprivation, the challenge of eliminating malnutrition in rural India through agriculture will probably keep me intellectually and emotionally occupied and satisfied for the remaining years of my life.

12

Conclusions

The Making of a Leader

What these stories and reminiscences demonstrate is a very particular style of leadership made up of several key components. First of all is a personal commitment to the cause of human dignity and social justice which forms the core philosophy of his life, driven by principles of trusteeship, secularism, inclusivity, equity and personal integrity. As a leader, this has enabled him to develop a sense of commitment amongst his colleagues, facilitating their personal and professional growth, and motivating them to work together and give their best to the common goal. Work then becomes a source of joy and satisfaction, rather than an onerous responsibility.

Second, while the leader is clearly one in command, the authority emerges from a position of knowledge from intellectual capacity, rather than hierarchy. It comes from generosity, from mentoring, from intellectual and personal support, rather than mere position. Respect is earned, not demanded. Alongside authority sits accountability Unfortunately accountability, as M.S. Swaminathan (MSS) says, "appears to be going out of our dictionary in India now, with people enjoying authority, centralising power in themselves, yet neither transparent nor accountable in their everyday practice."

A third key quality of a leader is the personal example of ethical behaviour, including a strong commitment to the organisational goals and to professional and personal ethics. Recognising collective contributions has meant that all the awards received by MSS over the years have been given to the M.S. Swaminathan Research Foundation (MSSRF), which today supports over 400 staff. Perhaps it reflects the Gandhian philosophy of trusteeship, that all property should serve the collective interest, especially of those who do not have it. Personal property inherited from the family was also given to the Foundation. His life has been one of simplicity, meeting basic needs, yet not coveting more than needed.

Fourth, a leader needs to recognise people and their contributions. In many places across the country, farmers, the poor, including women, remember his visits with fondness. This is because of a very personal quality—the willingness to speak to everyone, making sure that the cook, the driver, the watchman, etc., are all recognised and thanked for their service, making people feel valued for who they are. Once when he was Director General (DG) of International Rice Research Institute (IRRI), one of his two secretaries was on leave, so the other could not leave her seat to go for tea. He noticed this, and when he returned, had a packet in his hand for her—a little teacake which he had purchased in the cafeteria. She was very moved. If you love people and treat them as human beings, they love you back—relationships are always two-way and mutual. Little incidents like this stick in people's minds, and as they add up, they contribute to the making of a leader—a father figure who is truly cherished.

Fifth, while recognised as a giant in his field, he has remained open to new ideas, to debate and discussion, continuing to learn from life's everyday experiences. This is something I have experienced at close quarters—often we talk about something, and then he will ask me to write it down for him. He thinks about it and adapts it in his own way. And this is indeed a remarkable quality. We often feel that once we have said something or made a claim, we need to stick to our position. However, circumstances change, life changes, and one survives only through the willingness to adapt and learn. The Yield Revolution in wheat played a significant role in the country's history at that moment in time; yet over the years, he has taken on board many of the critiques, engaged with them, and developed new strategies in response. This openness and ability to learn needs to be highlighted, as many 'experts' today believe that they know it all!

Finally and perhaps most importantly, a leader has a vision, a message for the world. In MSS' case, following many years of varied experiences, this has been articulated in the mandate of the Foundation, a vision of equitable and sustainable development based on a pro-nature, pro-poor and pro- women stance. In 1994, Dr Gus Speth, the then head of United Nations Development Programme (UNDP), was invited to Pondicherry to inaugurate a threshing floor in one of the villages. He walked around the village, looking at activities of the women, almost unable to imagine how they lived and worked in those conditions. On his return to Delhi, he wrote a letter asking MSS if he could use the principles of 'pro-nature, pro-poor and pro-women' as part of UNDP's definition of human development. MSS replied, "When I do something, it is of local significance, when you do it, it assumes global significance. If you like this formulation, please do adopt it." Not many in UNDP know where this definition came from—the point really was not personal name or fame, but influencing the world of ideas and knowledge, both at the grass-roots and at the policy levels, in the cause of socially just development.

MSS' life has been an adventure in marrying science with societal needs, but equally developing methodologies and methods by which the livelihood security of local communities and the ecological security of the area can become mutually reinforcing—all with a very human and personal touch.

PART II

The Ethics and Politics of Science

Introduction

1. From Ship to Mouth to Right to Food: A 60-Year Journey
2. Grain Mountains and Hungry Millions: The Reality of Agrarian Distress
3. The Politics and Economics of Seeds
4. Integrated Planning and Management of Resources
5. Social, Demographic and Gender Dimensions of Science and Technology
6. Agricultural Research Strategies
7. Science and Public Policy

Introduction

One day in the late 1990s, an activist friend reminded me of the way things were in the 1960s and early 1970s. The drought in 1966 led to a Plan holiday for three consecutive years. India was forced to rely on food grains from abroad, especially wheat of inferior quality that came through the Public Law 480 (1954) scheme, and later the Food for Peace Act of 1966 from the United States (US). He spoke of long queues at the public distribution shops, how difficult it was for him and his family, who were essentially rice eaters, to start eating wheat. The then laws prohibited people from bringing rice from rural areas to Kolkata, but this led to a thriving rice smuggling ring that involved hundreds of village women bringing in small amounts of rice, hidden in their clothes, daily to the city.

Indeed, in 1965, P.V. Sukhatme, the then Director of the Food and Agriculture Organization's (FAO) Statistics Division, had written:

> *Between one half to two thirds of India's people do not get food of the right type, and between one quarter to one third do not even get enough quantity to eat in order to sustain a healthy active life. Add to this the staggering magnitude of malnutrition and actual hunger, the accelerating growth of population which even on a conservative assumption is expected to reach 625 million by 1980 and the one billion mark by 2000, and one has the colossal dimension of India's food problem (Sukhatme, 1965: 90).*

Yet today, India has achieved food self-sufficiency. In 2012, it was the world's largest rice exporter. At the same time, food stocks held by the Food Corporation of India (FCI), stood at 76 million tonnes, 138 per cent more than the stipulated 39 million tonnes buffer stock (Chandrasekhar, 2012). The National Food Security Act (2013) promises adequate food to every man, woman and child, based on home-grown food.

But while national food security has been achieved, many households remain food insecure. Food insecurity and malnutrition in India co-exist

with bulging domestic food grain facilities and strong export markets. There are more malnourished people in India than that in any other country in the world. In 2012, 217 million or 17.5 per cent of India's population was malnourished. Indeed, if the undernourished people in India constituted a single country, it would be the fifth most populous one in the world (Pritchard et al., 2013: 19).

The quest for explanations for how the transition from starvation to plenty took place and why hunger and malnourishment persists despite huge food grain surpluses had been bothering me for long. I finally decided to ask my father, M.S. Swaminathan (MSS), some hard questions about the history of agricultural science and its applications in India. I sought to capture his memories, but also probe the issue of the liabilities of scientists and the ethical dilemmas they face. I wanted to know the role of science in achieving the turn-around in food production. I felt that I had to ask if indeed he and his colleagues were culpable for the ills that came in the wake of the Green Revolution. From his responses, I felt that just as in Stanley Kramer's 1961 movie "Judgement at Nuremberg", scientists like judges are sometimes victims of politics—like justice, science too functions according to the whims and fancies of politics and politicians.

Several years ago, when he was President of Pugwash (2002-2007) and was visiting London, I accompanied him to meet the Nobel Laureate Joseph Rotblat. Rotblat had received the Nobel Peace Prize in 1995 along with the Pugwash Conferences on Science and World Affairs. Rotblat was deeply involved in the US government's Manhattan Project to develop an atomic bomb as a deterrent to rising Nazi power during the Second World War. When he realised that the bomb was actually going to be used in Japan, or against Russia, he resigned immediately. He was accused of being a Soviet spy, but was able to prove that all evidences against him were fabricated. He became an active leader of Pugwash (its Secretary-General from 1957-1973), the anti-nuclear movement started by Albert Einstein and Bertrand Russell, and the youngest signatory of the Russell-Einstein statement issued in 1955. The phrase: "Remember your humanity, and forget the rest", from this statement was quoted by Rotblat in his Nobel acceptance speech.

From my conversations with him, it seemed to me that it is this principle that has driven MSS in his life's work. Science is science, but his concern for humanity first has enabled MSS to stand up for the poor, the invisible, the excluded, going against the grain and even receiving flak, when it was strictly speaking not necessary for the performance of his job. His constant endeavour to make science work for farmers has meant taking on roles beyond the laboratory, actively seeking to engage with the political establishment and public policy. This journey has had its ups and downs, some of which I have captured in this book.

These conversations took place in the summer of 2014 when he and my mother visited me in Norwich where I teach at the University of East Anglia. Speaking to one's father, who is so eminent, is a daunting task and there is always a fear of either eulogising him or being overly critical. Moreover, I am a social scientist and do not have much idea about 'science', so I would often stop him in the middle of a conversation and ask him to explain concepts in simple lay terms, even at the risk of exasperating him. He helped me overcome that by being forthright and candid. Sometimes my mother, Mina, joined us. We discussed in-depth the role of the scientist in meeting societal challenges; whether science and technology itself is inherently inequitable; and what a scientist can do to minimise risk, while providing possible solutions to the problems confronting society. I wanted to know whether the nature of the scientific research environment and establishment has itself moved away from a focus on public good to private profit. I wanted to understand from him how to analyse the changes in India since Independence—a dramatic progress from 'ship to mouth to the right to food' on one hand, but accompanied by severe agrarian distress on the other.

Historians distinguish between history and memory. Though trained in History, I could not find an easy way to deal with the memories of someone like MSS who has shaped the history of agriculture and science in India over several decades. I let him talk freely and have compiled his views without juxtaposing mine or editing what he said.

1

From Ship to Mouth to Right to Food

A 60-Year Journey

Almost every country in the world has feted him and given him its highest honours and awards. He was elected Fellow of the Royal Society of London in 1973 and subsequently by the United States (US), Russian, Chinese and Italian Academies of Sciences. He has been named Commandeur of the Order of the Golden Ark of the Netherlands, and has received the Magsaysay Award for Community Leadership, the Ordre du Merite Agricole of France, and the Golden Heart Presidential Award of the Philippines. He has been awarded the Charles Darwin International Science and Environment Medal, the Volvo Environment Prize, the Tyler prize, the UNESCO Gandhi Gold Medal, the Franklin Delano Roosevelt Four Freedoms Medal, and the Indira Gandhi Prize for Peace, Disarmament and Development—to name just a few. The list goes on.

In 1987, he was the first recipient of the World Food Prize, considered equal to the Nobel Prize in the field of agriculture. With the US$ 200,000 that came with this prize, he started the M.S. Swaminathan Research Foundation (MSSRF) in Chennai. In 1999, Time magazine included him in its list of the 20 most influential Asians—the third Indian after Tagore and Gandhi.

In India, at the start of the Green Revolution, he received the Padma Shri in 1967. This was followed by the Padma Bhushan in 1972, and the Padma Vibhushan in 1989, in recognition of his scientific contributions to agriculture. He has not been awarded the Bharat Ratna, India's highest civilian award, much to our disappointment as well as that of his friends and admirers. In 2013, Gopal Gandhi wrote ruing this in the national daily, "The Hindustan Times" (26 November). Often a prophet is not recognised in his own country.

Receiving the first World Food Prize.

From what I have understood of him over the last five decades, I must say that he really doesn't hanker after awards and is stoically indifferent to praise or abuses. Awards aplenty have come his way, most of them recognising his unstinting service to India, working single-mindedly and with a deep sense of humanism, to ensure not just food security, but also food sovereignty at the national level. The films like Manoj Kumar's "Upkaar" in 1967, with its famous song 'mere deshki dharti sona ugle, ugle hirey moti' (Let the fields of my country spew gold, spew diamonds and pearls) idolised the soil and farmers, yet at that time the yields were low, nowhere near comparable to gold or precious stones. Faced with severe food crises, Prime Minister Lal Bahadur Shastri enjoined Indians to tighten their belts and miss a meal once a week.

But this became M.S. Swaminathan (MSS) challenge. He wanted to see this transformation happen in order to give meaning to slogans like 'jai jawan, jai kisan' by truly recognising the poor farmer. Replying to my

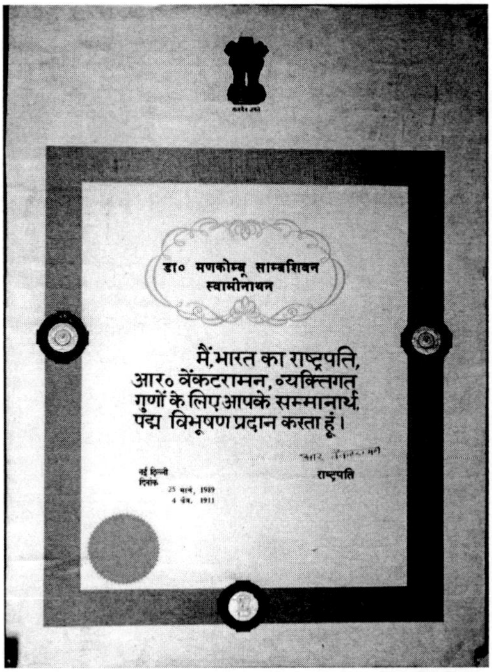

Padma Vibhushan.

question about the awards he has received, he told me that he considers his greatest award to be the warmth he has received from farmers, women and men, across the country—even their desire to share their simple meal with him. It is this sense of concern for people, especially the farmers, apart from his conviction that the prizes reflect joint work and contributions of many, which made him give all his prize money to the MS Swaminathan Research Foundation (MSSRF) so as to be used for public good research and development.

NR: *There is a lot written about Green Revolution and the technological breakthrough in yields. While not going into the details here, could you tell me briefly about your own scientific work, which formed the basis for many of the early awards and recognition you received?*

MSS: The Royal Society and many of the other awards recognised my contribution to theoretical and applied genetics which resulted in large yield increases. The theoretical contributions are related to my early original work on potato (1948-1953) and later work on wheat (1955-1970). In terms of application, I was recognised for breeding and popularising semi-dwarf varieties of wheat and rice.

In 1949, when I was in the Netherlands, Prof Toxopaeus at Wageningen University found that the most serious problem for potato cultivation was the golden nematode, a soil pathogen that attacks the roots and kills the plant. He asked whether I could help develop resistant lines, available only in wild varieties (*Solanum polyadeneum*) and not cultivated varieties (*Solanum tuberosum*). I tried, but was not successful in crossing these two as the pollen of one would not germinate on the stigma of the other. Anyway, I then left for Cambridge to do my PhD, where I had to work on the more basic aspects of the origin of potato. I wrote two papers in the *American Journal of Potato Research* (1952 and 1953). D.C. Cooper, R.W. Hougas and G.H. Reiman at the University of Wisconsin in Madison, US saw these papers and invited me to join them as a Research Associate in Genetics. I went to Wisconsin after completing my PhD viva in November 1952.

Wisconsin did not have the nematode problem, but one of frost due to very cold temperatures. There was a frost-resistant variety called *Solanum acaule*. I started crossing this with *S. tuberosum*, but had the same problem as in the Netherlands—it would not germinate. As I experimented, I decided to cut off the stigma, put an artificial stigma and then pollinate with *S. acaule*. This time it germinated. Between November 1952 and January 1954, I developed several crosses using this method. Bob Hougas and an Alaskan breeder later converted this into a variety, named Alaskan Frostless.

This method came to be called the 'Swaminathan artificial stigma method', where the medium is substitute for the stigma. In this method, the first step is surgery, to cut off the stigma and put an artificial medium. The next is hybridisation, that is to select the characteristic required and make the cross. We need to make a large number of crosses to get a few good varieties, as we cannot be sure if the cross will germinate successfully. Once it has germinated and has the desirable characteristics, tissue culture is then used to multiply it. This takes a few months, after which the seed can be taken to the farmer's fields.

In fact, when we were at Fitzwilliam House at the University of Cambridge in May this year (2014), the Master of the College reminded me that the records showed that I had a problem with landlady of the house in which I was staying. This was because I was often not able to return to the house in time for dinner at 6 pm. In the mornings I would go to the field to collect material for cytological

MSS and Mina with Bhaskar Vira and Nicola Padfield, Master of Fitzwilliam College, Cambridge, May 2014.

analysis and in the evening I would be in the laboratory conducting my experiments. If I was in the middle of making crosses, I could not leave it unfinished and go to the house in time for supper. The landlady could not appreciate my problem, and ultimately I shifted to the house of Moelwyn Hughes, Reader in Biochemistry. Mrs Hughes was very understanding and we parted as good friends.

In 1865, Gregor Mendel published his "Experiments in Plant Hybridisation". This paper was ignored for 35 years and rediscovered in 1900, as during that period, Darwinism and natural selection dominated the discourse. The period 1900-1953 was that of Mendelian breeding. In fact, one of the first awards I received was the Mendel Memorial Medal of the Czechoslovak Academy of Sciences in 1965 for contribution to plant genetics, in particular, using dwarfing genes from Mexican wheat varieties to produce our own HYVs (high yielding varieties) of wheat. My work was a major breakthrough. In 1953, Watson and Crick published their paper on the double helix structure of the DNA molecule; yet it took 30 years for the attention to shift to molecular breeding. This is a more precise method of breeding (genetic modification), though quite controversial now.

NR: *We will come back to the issue of seeds, as this seems central to your own contribution and the progress we have made in Indian agriculture. But first I would like to know a little about the political and human context of your work? I have read about the frequent droughts and the famines in colonial India. But as Amartya Sen has argued, famines are created by politics and not necessarily by food shortages.*

MSS: Famines were frequent in colonial India; in fact, most of the critical changes made in the agricultural administration during the colonial period came from the reports and recommendations of various famine commissions. The biggest famine had occured during World War II, the Bengal Famine of 1942-43, when several million children, women and men died of hunger. And even on the day of our Independence, newspapers reported shortage of food in the country to feed our 300 million people. Independent India became dependent on importing PL480 wheat from the US at concessional prices. Waiting for the ships carrying PL480 wheat to arrive before people could be fed came to be known as the 'Ship to Mouth' existence. At the international level, various doomsday predictions were made. Paul R. Ehrlich, in 1968, wrote *The Population Bomb*, where he said:

> Sometime between 1970 and 1985 the world will undergo vast famines—hundreds of millions of people are going to starve to death. That is, they will starve to death unless plague, thermonuclear war, or some other agent kills them first. The United States should announce that it will no longer ship food to countries such as India where dispassionate analysis indicates that the unbalance between food and population is hopeless.

Ehrlich endorsed the brothers, William and Paul Paddock's conclusion in their 1967 book, *Famine 1975–America's Decision: Who Will Survive* that India's capability to feed itself was hopeless. There was no future for India, they said and hence advised the US to stop giving us aid. It was in this context that we had to prove the prophets of doom wrong. Today we have the Right to Food, which gives each citizen the legal right to adequate food which is home-grown. It would not have been possible to enact such a strong social protection measure if the production was not sufficient, and available for procurement by the state. While the Green Revolution has its critics, without those early breakthroughs in yields, we would not have been where we are today in terms of food self-sufficiency as well as national sovereignty.

NR: *Several economists, including the Hungarian P.T. Bauer, challenged the population doomsdayers in his 1981 book "Equality, the Third World and Economic Delusion". Yet, there seemed inadequate attention to the production process itself, to the farmers and scientists involved in the agrarian transformations of the 1960s and 1970s. Can you tell me a little about the scientists and their ideologies and enthusiasm at that time?*

MSS: The farmers held a lot of knowledge. This needed to be combined with the work of scientists and the synergies unleashed to achieve a common goal. Yet in those days, there was little money for research. The laboratories were not well equipped. I remember in my own laboratory, as what was then called the Botany division of the Indian Agriculture Research Institute (IARI), there was only one good microscope. We all used to fight for it, and ultimately developed a system of reserving the microscope for one-hour slots during the day. But there was a lot of determination that we should get over the ignominy of being described as the nation which couldn't feed itself, whose farmers were lazy, fatalistic and unwilling to take up new technologies to improve productivity.

I recall Pandit Jawaharlal Nehru, in 1948, convening a meeting of Directors and Heads of Departments at IARI in order to understand the best way to overcome the problem of food shortage. His statement "everything else can wait but not agriculture" is often quoted. Many scientists were present there. I was a postgraduate student at that time, but because I was also the Secretary of the Postgraduate Union, I was asked to attend. Nehru said that the gap between demand and supply was only 10-15 per cent and therefore, it should not be difficult for India to achieve self-reliance in food. Nehru went round the table and everybody spoke about their own discipline and how it could solve the problem. The plant breeder said his variety would increase yield by 10-15 per cent. The entomologist maintained that by following his method of pest control, 20 per cent more yield could be obtained. The fertiliser expert claimed 15-20 per cent additional yield could be derived through the use of fertilisers. The rat control expert said that by killing rats, 30 per cent more production could easily be achieved. It all sounded so easy. Nehru joked and said, "If you do what everybody here is saying, you can double the production very quickly, so now what is the problem?" The problem was lack of coordination. It was clear that an inter-disciplinary approach was needed, scientists from different disciplines—pathology, entomology, agronomy, soil science, physiology and breeding—needed to come together, if progress was to be made. The message went home.

NR: *But did the other ministers in Nehru's cabinet share his vision?*

MSS: I joined the staff of IARI in 1955. We decided to do everything possible to ensure that India would be able to increase its production by enhancing productivity per unit area. This was not easy despite Nehru's faith in science and democracy, as some of his ministers had their own views. The Minister of Agriculture in 1958 didn't really value research. He asked all of us scientists to organise ourselves into brigades and go to the villages. Agriculture is a field where everyone thinks that he/she is an authority: that you don't have to learn, you don't to have to study, and you can just go to the fields and do something. We had to obey orders, but the villagers asked us for our suggestions. We were told to recommend a certain NP718 variety of wheat, but the seeds were not available, so the farmers lost interest.

NR: *So what did you learn from this experience?*

MSS: There were two invaluable lessons. First, the relationship between knowledge transfer and the inputs needed to apply that knowledge is very important; if these are not synchronised in time, credibility will be lost. Secondly, we need to marry brain with brawn; the farmers want us to bring technical knowledge, whether in water harvesting, mosquito control methods or seed varieties. They don't seek our physical labour. Incidentally, Gandhiji also gave this message to university students who wanted to do something for rural India. Rather than performing *shramdaan* a day or two in a year, he asked them to contribute their skills and knowledge for the upliftment of rural India. "Marry intellect with labour," he said.

NR: *And how did you marry brain and brawn?*

MSS: In 1963-64, we had some good seed varieties of wheat from Dr Norman Borlaug but no resources to produce them in large quantities. I proposed starting a 'Seed Village' near Delhi, but we had no money for this purpose. In fact, we used to go in our own car, and sometimes you children would also come. You all liked the Persian Wheel in some of the farmers' fields and considered the trip a Sunday picnic. The villagers were sceptical about what scientists and extension officers could offer, and refused to take up any intervention without subsidies. When I said there was no subsidy, but assured them the seeds would give them a good yield and better income, they were not convinced and demanded a subsidy. After two or three visits, one farmer in Jounti village, near Delhi, said, "Dr Saab, we will take up your seed." I asked why he had changed his mind. He said, "You people are coming on a Sunday, on holidays; this means you are not being paid for this, otherwise you would have come only on working days. It is not your regular job." They are observant and in this case more than our talk, it was the non-verbal communication that convinced them

In the field.

to try the seeds. Each one of us wants to be treated with respect. We should not therefore underestimate their knowledge of their farms or capacity to interpret human interactions. Of course, later they became very prosperous as they could sell the seeds at high prices.

We didn't have money, we didn't have staff, but at this point, the students came forward. Venkatrao Gadwal (now Adviser Mahyco) and later B. Venkateswarlu (later Director of the Central Rice Research Institute, Cuttack) were then Presidents of the Students' Union and they mobilised several students to help us in the field. So whether it was a student, a scientist, or a research assistant, it didn't matter. It was what I called a symphony; everybody had a role to play and they all came forward together and put their heart and soul into the work. Today when I look back, I don't know how it happened, but the fact remains that the success was because of the enormous enthusiasm of scientists and farmers, and of students and staff.

NR: *The ambience in those days must have been very challenging but at the same time exciting.*

MSS: When there is a challenge, it also works as an opportunity to achieve and move ahead. Many important scientific discoveries were made during the two world wars. Probably that is what happened in those days. Our salaries were low and I earned ₹ 450 per month; but the cost of living was also low. In any case, we didn't look at the money, but rather at the opportunity for breaking the doomsday predictions of the Paddock brothers and the Ehrlichs. Just around that time (1967-68), we were on the verge of a yield breakthrough in wheat. It was really a remarkable period where I should say the scientific dedication, scientific determination and scientific concentration on a particular objective, to overcome the particular problem of hunger, motivated us to give our best. Nothing special was given by the government to scientists, though farmers were given incentives such as subsidised fertilisers; the Food Corporation of India (FCI) was set up to procure surplus grain and the Agriculture Prices Commission was set up to fix minimum support prices. I was given the Padma Shri in 1967, and the citation recognises the contribution towards creating 'a new confidence in India's agriculture capability'. There was appreciation and encouragement by politicians such as Shri C. Subramaniam, Jagjivan Ram (Ministers of Agriculture) and the Prime Ministers of that time, but they could not do much for us monetarily—neither in terms of our salaries nor laboratories.

NR: *But what about recognising the real contributors, that is the farmers? Did you make any efforts to ensure that they got the necessary recognition?*

MSS: From 1961 to 1965, I was head of the Botany division at IARI. Just as scientists were given recognition, we wanted to give social recognition and prestige to farmers as well. I suggested to Pandya from Gujarat, who was leading a farmer's organisation, that we should think of some way of recognising farmers for their yield consciousness. Several groups got together and suggested the formation of a National Tonnage Club for farmers, with a one tonne per hectare yield-oriented target for membership, as a counter to the Rotary and other clubs for the elites. Shri C. Subramaniam agreed to inaugurate the club and give it his blessings. It was launched in 1965 outside the Vidhan Sabha in Bhopal. This made farmers proud of their achievement.

Now we speak of recognition to women farmers. At that time, any farmer, even a man, was not considered knowledgeable or intelligent enough to take to new technology. We had to also enhance their self-esteem as farmers. A series of activities were started—National Demonstrations on farmers' fields, the use of radio, the National Tonnage Club—giving them specialist skills and status like seed producers in order to upgrade their technological competence as well as pride as farmers. Some of these were voluntary activities, for some we received support from the government, and for others developed partnerships—one of the most fruitful perhaps was with the Atomic Energy Commission. These strategies were time-specific. Today the Tonnage Club, for instance, is not relevant, as farmers produce much more, but other ways need to be found. The lesson really is that technology is important, but not enough. The self-esteem and attitudes of human beings behind the technology are critical. This comes with some encouragement and recognition.

NR: *How did you actually show the farmers that change was possible? How did you garner resources for this?*

MSS: When I became Director of IARI in 1966, our farm was in bad shape. The first thing I did was to attend to its improvement because I felt that if our own farm does not have good crops, what do we tell the farmers? It must be an example to others. While we had got some equipment through allocations from the Five Year Plans, I developed a collaborative relationship with the Rockefeller Foundation. Guy Baird, who was the field director of the Indian Agriculture Programme in New Delhi, gave us adequate farm equipment, particularly tractors, and helped to set up the Department of Farm Management. They also gave us an irradiation machine. We also started *Krishi Melas* twice a year—one during the *kharif* season and another during *rabi*. These became very popular among farmers.

The most satisfying partnership perhaps was the one with the Atomic Energy Commission. My first PhD student A.T. Natarajan, and later P.C. Kesavan, did some excellent work in the field of radiation-induced mutations. We had started this work on mutation breeding through radiation biology in 1955 itself. I went to Trombay and met Raja Ramanna who was head of the Radiation Physics Department there. He took me to meet Homi Bhabha. When I explained what we wanted to do, Bhabha was very impressed and put me on the team to go to the 2nd UN Conference on Peaceful Use of Atomic Energy at Geneva in 1958. I presented a keynote paper on the theme of neutron radiation, jointly with Natarajan. The idea was to expose the seed to radiation to create a mutation. This does not do any harm and the impacts are short-term—importers, for instance, want only irradiated mango, so the mango weevil is destroyed in the short-term. This began an excellent era of collaboration.

Apart from the use of radiation (X-rays, gamma rays, and fast and thermal neutrons), a second method of creating mutations is through chemical mutagenesis. During the Second World War, Dr Charlotte Auerbach found nerve gases, called 'mustard gas', which caused

Working in the lab, IARI.

mutations. She came to IARI in the early 1960s and worked with some of my students like V.L. Chopra. We needed chemicals for this. Luckily for us, Bjorn Sigurbjornsson, Head of the International Atomic Energy Agency at that time, gave us small funds of 1,000 or 2,000 US dollars. This seems small now, but was *manna* to us then. There was a resource crunch, but then we used the available resources much more carefully—you try and optimise the benefits of whatever you have. Now there are lavish buildings and expensive equipment, but these are taken for granted.

NR: *Could you tell me a little more about your collaboration with the Atomic Energy Commission, especially Vikram Sarabhai?*

MSS: I would really like to pay tribute to Vikram Sarabhai here. Following Homi Bhabha's sudden death in an air crash in 1966 en route to Geneva, Vikram became the Director of Atomic Energy Centre and then renamed it as Bhabha Atomic Research Centre. Vikram and I had a very close relationship. I would like to mention two incidents that I remember vividly, but which were also transformative in terms of science in India.

When I was Director of IARI in 1968, there was a complaint about the root wilt disease in coconut trees in the Kollam area of Kerala. Vikram suggested that we could hire remote sensing equipment, not available or used in India at that time, from the National Aeronautical and Space Agency (NASA) of the US in order to identify if the root wilt was spreading or confined to a particular area. I went to Indira Gandhi, the then Prime Minister, and asked her for permission to approach NASA for hiring the equipment. At that time, the Communist Party of India (Marxist) [CPI(M)] was in power in Kerala and Achyuta Menon was the Chief Minister. She said that I should ask him, as he might not be willing to collaborate with NASA. As this disease was a big problem in Kerala, Menon agreed. Vikram then approached NASA and organised the hiring of equipment—cameras, aircraft and personnel. Each plant has a spectral signature, which varies between the healthy and diseased plants. The photographs showed us that the root wilt was confined by the River Chalakudi to the Kollam area in Travancore. C.

With Indira Gandhi and Jagjivan Ram (centre) at IARI.

Dakshinamurthy, Head of the Physics Department at IARI, handled this project. This was the very first instance of remote sensing in India, and following this experience, the Government of India invested in remote sensing equipment. As far as the coconuts were concerned, it was hard to find resistant varieties, and ultimately many of the trees had to be cut down.

A second fruitful collaboration was the setting up of the Nuclear Research Laboratory (NRL) at IARI. I secured funds for the building through a United Nations Development Programme (UNDP) project. In those days, we could not use private builders, so I sent an architect from the Public Works Department (PWD) to Trombay in order to develop a suitable design for the laboratory. In December 1971, India was on the verge of war with Pakistan over the independence of Bangladesh. In any case, we decided to inaugurate the building, and invited Indira Gandhi, the then Prime Minister. Vikram also came. I had arranged for the labour involved in constructing the building to gather in a tent to meet Mrs Gandhi. As I led her there, she asked if they knew what the building was for. I said that they probably didn't, so she explained to them that the laboratory would be used to develop better varieties of food grains, pulses and other crops. The NRL greatly enhanced the research facilities available to Indian agricultural scientists.

After the function, I went with Vikram to Ashoka Hotel where he was staying. We had dinner together. Next morning he left for Trivandrum. The following morning I received a call from his wife Mrinalini to say that Vikram had died in the hotel in Trivandrum the previous night. It was a great loss. He was a very fine man.

NR: *By the early 1970s, you were quite well recognised. Did you not get any lucrative offers abroad?*

MSS: In 1971, before B.P. Pal retired as Director General (DG), Indian Council of Agricultural Research (ICAR), one day, Fakhrudin Ali Ahmed, the then Minister of Agriculture, called me and said that the government had set up a search committee headed by Vikram Sarabhai, and they had unanimously recommended that I should be invited to be the next DG of ICAR. I said that I was prepared to do whatever I could for the country. At the same time, Mr Boerma, the then DG, Food and Agriculture Organization (FAO), Rome, called Fakhrudin Ahmed and said, "We want Swaminathan to come to Rome as Assistant Director General, Agriculture." Ahmed telephoned me and said that he was under pressure to relieve me, as India didn't have any senior positions at the FAO. He said it was an honour for the country. Without even waiting to think, I spontaneously said that going to FAO at this time was out of the question for me. The salaries and the position might be high, but there was still a lot of work that needed to be done in India. So I refused. Boerma himself rang me up but I did not change my position.

NR: *Despite all the frustrations of those days, lack of resources for research included, what made you stay on in India?*

MSS: I think the main reason for staying on was work satisfaction. If you are frustrated, then you would jump at getting a foreign position. Though my salary was low, maybe ₹ 1300 per month, in contrast to probably over 7,000 US dollars at FAO, I did not even think of this as an option. I was working with scientists, with farmers in the field, and with policy makers, and at all levels, people were receptive and enthusiastic. It was not merely talking and writing long reports; we acted and showed in practice that we were not mouthing empty words. Without this job satisfaction, I might have shifted.

In fact, probably this was what happened in 1981, when I accepted the post of DG, International Rice Research Institute (IRRI). I was then in the Planning Commission, holding meetings all day, writing reports, yet no action was taken, there was no implementation on the ground. So I felt it was better to go back to research. In retrospect, I feel it was a wise decision at that stage in my career as it enlarged my understanding of agriculture in Asia. It certainly helped me in my future work in India.

Incidentally, that was not the first time I got a job offer from abroad. I had got two such offers earlier but I was not interested because since my college days, I wanted to do something for my country and the poor farmers. When I was working at Wisconsin in 1953, the first job offer came from the Red Dot Potato Chip Company to develop a high specific gravity potato variety for their products. That is an interesting story. During the Great Depression, Miller and his wife were both studying for their PhDs at Wisconsin, but with the Depression, they could not afford to pay their fees. So Mrs Miller gave up her studies and set up a business, selling potato chips outside pubs. She supported her husband with his PhD. When the Depression was over, they formed a chip company and wanted a good variety of potato. They contacted me and in fact took me to their farm in their private plane, and offered me a job. But I refused, as my intention was never to stay there. Later the University of Wisconsin also offered me a regular job in the Genetics Department, but I refused. I didn't really want to develop varieties myself, rather I wanted to develop novel genetic material/combinations and give it to the breeder. I was interested in pre-breeding.

NR: *What would you then say were the essential ingredients of the agricultural transformation?*

MSS: Looking back, there were three important factors behind this transformation from ship-to-mouth to food security as a right. Firstly, the Nehru era marked the development of the scientific infrastructure essential for improving farm productivity, such as major and minor irrigation projects, fertiliser factories, agricultural universities, farm extension services and marketing facilities. To benefit from the investment made in these areas, an Intensive Agricultural District Programme (IADP) was started in 1960-61. By 1963-64, IADP had covered 15 districts. Unfortunately, the impact of IADP on yield improvement was not up to expectation.

My analysis showed that the package of practices missed one important ingredient, namely, a genetic strain which could respond to the rest of the package, particularly irrigation water and fertiliser. Our own varieties could not absorb adequate fertiliser, and if applied, would fall down, a process called 'lodging'. Having identified the scientific intervention needed to break the yield stalemate, we initiated a search for suitable genes to create a short variety that could respond to soil fertility. The new plant architecture helped convert nutrients and water more efficiently into grains.

The second transformational factor was procurement of food grains from farmers at a minimum support price fixed on the advice of the Agricultural Prices Commission (APC). A small government programme titled "High Yielding Varieties Programme" became a mass movement owing to the enthusiasm generated among farm families both by the yield revolution, and the opportunities for assured and remunerative marketing. Wheat production has continued to rise since 1968 and has now reached a level of 92 million tonnes.

A third but very critical factor was the synergy between scientific know-how, political do-how and farmers' toil—often referred to as the 'Green Revolution symphony'. I have always called the Green Revolution a symphony of four ingredients. One is science which is the prime mover of change, another the gamut of public policies, particularly pricing, purchase, minimum support price and procurement of surplus produce; third is services such as seed production, electricity and fertiliser; and finally, farmers' enthusiasm. In 1968, a special stamp was released to commemorate what was called the Wheat Revolution. The library clock tower at Pusa Institute (IARI) figured on the stamp, a mark of the impact of science. A library is after all a symbol of knowledge and therefore a symbol of science. In fact, the text acknowledged that this was a science-induced 'revolution', wherein the contributions of the scientists behind it must be honoured and recognised.

A Focus on People: Combining Responsibility, Authority and Accountability

NR: *During doctoral research in Jharkhand in the late 1990s, living in two Santal villages, I learnt many lessons from Santal women there. Despite material poverty, what was important to them was their sense of dignity. They wanted to be treated and recognised as thinking, intellectual beings, rather than 'marginalised', 'poor', waiting for solutions to be delivered to them by the State and NGOs. It is only later that I discovered that you had been practising this principle at least from the 1960s, and had never hesitated to struggle for the dignity of farmers, men and women alike. As a scientist, how did you develop this insight and what changes could you bring about in the way things functioned?*

MSS: Being in the field of agriculture, I used to spend a lot of time in villages, talking to people, observing what they did, listening to what they said. This has shaped much of my thinking, as I realised that whatever I did must touch the lives of the poorest farm men and women in the country. There have been many impediments and difficulties, but I have always felt my responsibility to be towards the farmers and farm labourers in this country.

In IARI, when I was Director, there were many farm workers, 300-400 *beldars* (labourers), who were all permanently 'temporary'. There was a rule in government that if somebody is employed continuously for 220 days, they have to be made regular/permanent staff. It was not possible to resolve this issue, so I went to the then Finance Minister, quoted the rules, and he approved the regularisation. One needs courage and concern, but also proper knowledge of the rules and procedures to work out the best solutions.

It was during Subramaniam's time that an agricultural scientist, B.P. Pal, was made the DG of ICAR, until then he was a bureaucrat. Subramaniam recognised the contribution made by scientists and technically informed people to the Ministry. Following Homi Bhabha's model of combining scientific and administrative authority (he was himself the Chairman of the Atomic Energy Commission and at the same time Secretary to the Department of Atomic Energy), the Department of Agricultural Research and Education (DARE) was set up in 1974 with the DG, ICAR, as Secretary. This was vital as it made scientific principles the basis of administrative procedures. I remember when the proposal for DARE came up, the Minister and Secretary of Education opposed it, as they believed all higher education institutions including Agricultural Universities should fall under the purview of the University Grants Commission (UGC). I put up a Cabinet note explaining how the agricultural universities were being supported by ICAR, hence asked that DARE be allowed to retain three inter-connected functions—education, research and extension. The UGC could have representation on the Board of DARE. Indira Gandhi, the then Prime Minister, saw the sense in this and agreed.

As DG, ICAR and Secretary, DARE, I could directly prepare Cabinet notes or go to the Planning Commission with projects. Speedy decisions were taken as there was no mediation required. I had wanted the same for the DG, Indian Council of Medical Research (ICMR) and the DG, Indian Meteorological Department (IMD). Monsoon predictions are so important for agriculture, yet it became a political issue; if the predictions were bad, the ministers would ask for it not to be announced. Whatever it be, early warning can help farmers take measures to reduce their risks. But of course, while the system is in place, how this authority is exercised depends on the person as well. In recent years, it is unfortunate that the close coordination between education and research has become weak, and so the value and role of scientific insights have declined in the administration of agricultural research and education. Somewhere the link between having authority, and responsibility and accountability to the farmers of this country, seems to be broken. In the dairy sector, V. Kurien was strongly committed to the principle of accountability to farmers. This helped us climb to the number one position in the world in milk production.

NR: *What about the 'political will' and the policy commitment? How have things changed today?*

MSS: What we do is shaped by our environment—the scientific challenge before us was very great in the 1960s. The political atmosphere was conducive in the sense that the political leaders were willing to listen, and the general public atmosphere, including the media, was also encouraging and supportive. Today, there are a number of scientific committees, but the young, creative people don't find a voice in them. When addressing the annual meeting of ICAR recently, I emphasised that we need to give priority to brains and not bricks. Beautiful buildings are constructed, but there are hardly any good people in them. Complacency seems to have set in amongst both the political leadership and scientists, as there is so much grain in our go-downs. Yet if one looks at the storage, it is sad because a lot of grains are rotting. According to non-official estimates, grain losses are as high as 10-15 per cent. I have frequently said that while the Right to Information[1] can be implemented with the help of files, the Right to Food[2] can be implemented only with the help of farmers. And farmers' problems are growing.

Maybe it is due to this complacency that scientists are not able to speak. In the days of Nehru, Subramaniam, Jagjivan Ram and Surjit Singh Barnala (agriculture ministers during the 1970s), we could speak freely, we could criticise the government, we could point out what was wrong or right. But we didn't just critique, we also gave concrete suggestions based on our research and field realities. That interaction between the scientists and political leaders has declined, and administrators have gained the upper hand. Most of the jobs in the Agriculture Ministry are now held by non-specialists, and despite

---

1. Right to Information Act 2005 mandates timely response to citizen requests for government information *(http://rti.gov.in/)*.
2. The National Food Security Act 2013, provides for food and nutritional security with a human life cycle approach, by ensuring access to adequate quantity of quality food at affordable prices to people to live a life with dignity. *(http://indiacode.nic.in/acts-in-pdf/202013.pdf)*.

being good administrators, they are not sensitive to farmers' needs. Government servants have a Pay Commission, which adjusts their incomes to inflation and costs of living, but there is no Pay Commission for the farmers. Scientists too have a very indifferent attitude; they don't see it as their responsibility to convince the political administration and try and change their views. I recall Dr D.P. Singh, former Vice Chancellor of one of the first agricultural universities in India, located in Pantnagar (now in Uttarakhand), telling me that he always carried his resignation letter in his pocket. If at any time he felt that the Minister was not providing support in developing the University, he would hand over the letter. That kind of attitude and the desire to maintain dignity of the scientific establishment are hard to find today.

Every year before the budget, the Finance Minister still asks me for a note on what can be done for farmers and for agriculture. Pranab Mukherjee, while being the Finance Minister, was convinced about the Mahila Kisan Sashaktikaran Pariyojana (MKSP),[3] and had put some money into the budget; similarly P. Chidambaram, as Finance Minister provided an allocation for starting 'nutri-farms' last year (2013). But this is due to my own personal credibility. These ideas are not coming from scientists through the Agriculture Ministry. The downside then is the lack of implementation.

NR: *How do you think the communication between scientists and the political leadership can be revived?*

MSS: Every scientific organisation must have a committee to enhance the political and public understanding of science. The Royal Society of London has two such committees. I remember several years ago, when the discussion on climate change was emerging, the then Prime Minister of Britain, Margaret Thatcher, was very sceptical. Senior scientists and Fellows of the Royal Society arranged a full-day briefing for her. They provided her with both scientific and educational

3. The MKSP, a sub-component of the National Rural Livelihoods Mission, seeks to improve the capacities of women in agriculture to access resources from other institutions and schemes within a convergence framework (*www.mksp.in/*).

materials and convinced her of the need to give serious consideration to the issue.

In the 1950s and 1960s, we had leaders like Homi Bhabha and Shanti Swarup Bhatnagar (the then Vice President of the Council for Scientific and Industrial Research), who advised Nehru on matters of science. Many national laboratories were set up. Bhabha realised the importance of skilled manpower, physicists of the highest calibre, to deal with the new challenges and opportunities created by the use of nuclear power; hence, he secured support from J.R.D. Tata to set up the Tata Institute of Fundamental Research. They had tremendous credibility and their words carried conviction with the political leaders. While I should not praise myself, the fact remains that during the 1960s and 1970s, I had considerable influence on public policy related to agriculture, mainly because of my credibility, but also the trust and friendship developed with political leaders. At times, they took the initiative and we scientists had to implement; and at others, we proposed ideas to meet new challenges, gave concrete suggestions, and they provided the necessary public policy support.

Given the breakdown in such a working relationship, I recommended to the National Academy of Agricultural Sciences to set up a committee on the political understanding of science, similar to the Royal Society, to deal with important issues such as genetic modification. There are public apprehensions, especially around health and safety implications of genetically modified (GM) crops. Can GM crops be used in a safe and responsible manner? I don't worship or discard any technology outright; the technology itself is neither safe nor unsafe. We need to understand the purpose and use of the particular technology and the risks entailed. These issues need to be debated and discussed in the spirit of science.

Many chief ministers of Indian states have declared their states as organic farming ones, without understanding the implication of organic farming. Organic farming requires more research than chemical farming, as you cannot use chemicals to restore and maintain soil health, control plant diseases, and the triple alliance of pests, pathogens and weeds. So how does one use organic farming to produce more from limited land, to feed the growing population of the country, to meet the commitments of the Food Security Act?

Our soils are hungry and thirsty; the plant needs nutrients to provide yields, it doesn't distinguish between organic manure and chemical fertiliser. To produce one tonne of wheat, the plant requires 25 kg of nitrogen, the source doesn't matter. How many cows or buffaloes does a small farmer have? Where is the manure going to come from? Do we have other forms of organic manure such as vermi-compost in adequate amounts? These are scientific issues, and I think scientists have to take responsibility for allaying apprehensions so as to make politicians understand the implications of policy, presenting them with alternatives, rather than staying silent. A recent editorial in *Science* notes: "Scientists that know how to talk to Congress are worth their weight in gold" (Carney, 18 July 2014).

What are the options available? One option could be to create an integrated nutrient supply and integrated pest management system, where the application of chemical fertilisers and pesticides is minimised, focusing instead on organic and green manure and bio-fertilisers, to the extent that they are available. Scientists in ICAR and agricultural universities have this knowledge, but are not speaking out. They do not present the pros and cons in a way that the public can understand. They are probably afraid that if they speak, they will be called agents of fertiliser or pesticide companies. But it is important to present a balance sheet of our obligations to feed the nation, alongside preventing ecological harm, as there are scientific, public policy, economic and food security issues involved. We cannot really afford to experiment with the lives of the poor in this country.

A further problem with our scientific establishment is that it is divided, with little coordination among agencies. They don't work together, hence the impact is much lower than what it could be. What we need is leadership at two levels—scientific leadership and political leadership that is supportive of science. A missing ingredient today is the enthusiasm and determination of our scientists to take our country forward. The Chinese have it. The Chinese Academy of Agriculture Sciences is engaged with systematically identifying the challenges of the future, such as climate change, population pressure on land and working out solutions. No one is called landless—people are either in farm-based or non-farm-based employment. We too need a positive attitude; the self-confidence and determination to confront our present challenges. The main problem seems to be a neglect of the human aspect, brushing the crises facing farmers' today under the carpet, rather than finding creative solutions.

2

Grain Mountains and Hungry Millions

The Reality of Agrarian Distress

NR: *While there is sufficient food production now, we find that inequalities have increased between the rural and urban. Many small and marginal farmers are forced to migrate to the towns to earn a living as rickshaw pullers or other manual workers. Santals and other tribal groups from Jharkhand work as agricultural labour in the sugar cane fields of western Uttar Pradesh, or in the construction of border roads, year after year, despite owning land at home. Extension services elude them; they are not seen as motivated because they are unable to pay the costs of transportation to travel for extension meetings and demonstrations.*

Farmer suicides have increased over the last decade. According to the National Crime Records Bureau, more than 10 per cent of all recorded suicides between 2010 and 2012, that is, roughly 14,000-15,000 per year, has been that of farmers. Clearly the reality is one of agrarian distress. How and why do you think this has happened, after the euphoria of the 1960s and the 1970s?

MSS: A major cause, I think, is the failure of technology and its costs for the poor. The failure of social support systems is yet another major cause. Let me elaborate.

Farming is a life-giving profession. If farmers take their own lives, then there is something radically wrong with our society. The data show the growing impoverishment of farmers. They constitute 60 per cent of our people, but the contribution of agriculture to GDP (gross domestic product) has come down to about 14 per cent; that means the average income of these farmers is quite low. While there are a few studies which see failure of the institutional credit system, and dependence on usurious informal credit as the major reasons for agrarian distress, I feel there must be something more profound at

Moving out for work.

work. There are many packages for the Vidarbha farmers (the eastern region of the state of Maharashtra comprising Amravati and Nagpur divisions), but they don't seem to be addressing the root of the problem.

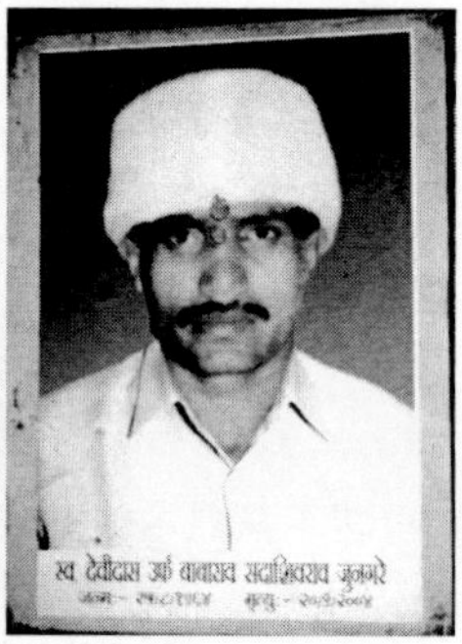

Agrarian distress has always existed in our country. In the past, it was linked very strongly to monsoon behaviour, as only 10-12 per cent of the land was irrigated. Rains failed regularly, and it was to confront this that the then British government introduced the Famine Codes and the Famine Commissions. As soon as a famine was announced, rural works programmes would be initiated.

Today farmers too have aspirations. They need higher incomes, and to enhance incomes they adopt new technologies. Many of the

Packet of hybrid cotton seed.

farmers who committed suicide in Vidarbha had taken to Bt cotton and other advanced technologies. These are expensive, and their coping capacity is limited; so if the monsoon as well as the technology fails, they are in dire straits. In my 2004 Report of the Taskforce on Applications of Agricultural Biotechnology to the Ministry of Agriculture, I had recommended that companies should insulate farmers against failure of technology, say Bt cotton seeds, for reasons beyond their control. Technology insurance is particularly important for such high-risk, high-cost technologies. Unlike high-yielding varieties (HYVs), hybrid seeds have to be purchased every year by the farmers. Companies should pay the premium for this insurance as part of their mandatory contributions to corporate social responsibility (CSR). They are making profits from selling these seeds to very poor people, hence should also have some responsibility for alleviating possible distress.

Another aspect about the suicides has always worried me. Born in a joint family, I have witnessed a lot of support within the family. My father died young, but my father's brother looked after us. When I was Chairman of the Farmers' Commission (2004-2006), we went from village to village, and I asked *panchayat* leaders about the suicides. Surely they knew about the families in distress, those who were indebted. Did they not have any social protection system to prevent these suicides? Everything cannot be left to the government. I was saddened to see that the sense of community, of local support and responsibility has also declined. The Farmers' Commission

Wilted and abandoned: Cotton field in Vidarbha.

recommended empowering the *panchayat* to identify cases of distress and providing some timely local support.

Finally in the 1960s, there was more unified support to farmers, looking at the totality of needs and requirements, not just technology, but also irrigation, rural infrastructure and marketing facilities. After the 1960s, the Ministry of Agriculture was gradually sub-divided into a number of ministries—land went to Rural Development, storage and post-harvest technology to the Ministry of Food, fertilisers and pesticides to the Ministry of Chemicals, irrigation to the Ministry of Water Resources, and so on. With so many ministries, collaboration is important if you want to "deliver as one", to use UN Secretary General Ban Ki Moon's phrase. For agricultural reform, what is needed is the integrated and coordinated delivery of services to the farmers. With fragmentation of the responsibilities, there is no accountability to the farmer. The lack of accountability too has contributed towards intensifying distress.

In fact, the key recommendations of the National Commission for Farmers[1] are included in the National Policy for Farmers (*http://agricoop.nic.in/NPF/npff2007.pdf*). It called for a 'paradigm shift'—the need to improve economic viability of farming by substantially increasing the income of farmers, not just the yield per hectare. This would imply attention to input prices, remunerative marketing and access to technology designed to add value to primary products. The farmers at present have no control over the process, neither the inputs nor the markets.

NR: *Do you think there is a problem with the new technologies per se, or is it the collapse of the public extension and information system that has contributed to the distress?*

MSS: Technology has two faces, it can be empowering, leading to an improvement in quality of life, but it can also lead to distress. In rainfed areas like Vidarbha or Telengana, Bt cotton technology should never have been promoted without adequate technological protection and safeguards like insurance. Traditionally, farmers here grew castor and pulses (pigeon pea). These can survive in drought conditions. They also have a good market price. Loan waivers may be a short-term solution, but they don't address the basic problem—of crop choices, of rainwater harvesting and of alternate fodder for cattle. Gujarat achieved agricultural growth mainly due to assured irrigation from the Narmada, combined with protected, hi-tech (greenhouse) agriculture; whereas Thanjavur (a district in Tamil Nadu) farmers are in distress because the availability of Cauveri (river) water is slowly declining, and the water table is going down, making filter point irrigation difficult. We need proactive rather than reactive strategies, and this requires a responsible public extension system.

Today the extension services have gone down in both quantity and quality, as recognised also by the Planning Commission's Working Group on Agricultural Extension (2007). The World Bank initiated the

1. The National Commission on Farmers submitted five reports over the period of December 2004 to October 2006. Following from the first four, the final report focused on causes of farmer distress and the rise in farmer suicides, and recommended addressing them through a holistic national policy for farmers. The findings and recommendations encompass issues of access to resources and social security entitlements (*http://www.kisanayog.gov.in/*).

Declining levels of water.

Training and Visit system in the 1970s. This proved a failure and was replaced by the Agriculture Technology Management Agency (ATMA).[2] While good in theory, it has many limitations in real life, including being headed by the District Collector, who has no time for it amongst his/her many responsibilities. Companies have become the main source of information, and driven as they are by the profit motive, they give a lot of propaganda to these seeds. They don't advice farmers on the risks involved in rainfed areas, nor do they provide insurance cover as I have suggested.

Of course, farmers will be tempted by the thought of increased earnings. While they know that the crops may not survive, they take up technologies for which the market price is attractive. Similarly, crops like sugar cane should not be promoted in water-short areas; yet in Maharashtra, this is a political crop promoted by a strong sugar cane lobby, rather than a crop of scientific choice. This is where the courage of the extension officers and the agricultural universities is needed,

2. A district-level body, whose main aim is to identify location-specific needs of farming communities for farming system-based agricultural development.

to tell farmers the truth, but they don't point out the risks, especially when political interests are at stake. The long-term implications of inappropriate land use and crop choice are seldom pointed out.

The dwarf wheat too spread like wildfire in the late 1960s (1965-1968), as the farmer getting one tonne could now get four to five tonnes per hectare. But we only promoted it in areas with assured irrigation in order to minimise risks to the farmers. Of course, this is also a critique of the Green Revolution, but it never led to the kind of distress we see today. The difference was that it was a Government programme which became a mass movement, and information on risks and benefits was provided by public institutions as there was no direct profit motive. I think this is where the role of public good research and public extension institutions needs to be emphasised. In fact, as early as in 1968, in my address to the Indian Science Congress held at Varanasi, I had pointed to the risks of intensifying agriculture without fully understanding the consequences of our interventions. I had said then:

> Intensive cultivation of land without conservation of soil fertility and soil structure would lead ultimately to the springing up of deserts. Irrigation without arrangements for drainage would result in soils getting alkaline or saline. Indiscriminate use of pesticides, fungicides and herbicides could cause adverse changes in biological balance as well as lead to an increase in the incidence of cancer and other diseases, through the toxic residues present in the grains or other edible parts. Unscientific tapping of underground water would lead to the rapid exhaustion of this wonderful capital resource left to us through ages of natural farming. The rapid replacement of numerous locally adapted varieties with one or two high yielding strains in large contiguous areas would result in the spread of serious diseases capable of wiping out entire crops, as happened prior to the Irish potato famine of 1845 and the Bengal rice famine of 1942. Therefore, the initiation of exploitative agriculture without a proper understanding of the various consequences of every one of the changes introduced into traditional agriculture, and without first building up a

> proper scientific and training base to sustain it, may only lead us into an era of agricultural disaster in the long run, rather than to an era of agricultural prosperity (4 January 1968).

If equity is put first, then one should really prioritise work in harsh environments like deserts or mountain areas. The more difficult the problem, the more attention is needed to find solutions. We do have good technologies for *barani* or dry land cultivation, the All India Dryland Farming project was initiated, and the International Crops Research Institute for the Semi-Arid Tropics (ICRISAT) was set up, but the problem has been their inability to take it to the field due to poor extension. I suggested in the Report of the National Farmers' Commission that the Directors of Agricultural Extension should be outstanding farmers, who understand the problems of farmers and farming and not bureaucrats. Unfortunately, a well-informed scientific extension system has been replaced by the private sector, seed and fertiliser companies, who are advising farmers on what to do or not to do. Modern technologies can help overcome problems as our Village Knowledge Centres (VKCs) have demonstrated; however, these solutions are not being put forward.

NR: *Have changing aspirations also contributed to the distress?*

MSS: From 1990, with the opening up of the economy, it is true that there has been an enlargement of opportunities for young people in the services sector. Agriculture requires a lot of services—pest-proofing of whole villages, post-harvest management, value addition—yet no attention has been given to developing and supporting these services; the focus has been on export-oriented IT (information technology). Small farmers are not able to earn enough in the absence of services which can provide them with the power and economy of scale; they are beholden to the vagaries of monsoon and markets, and fall into serious debt traps.

The problem has become more intense as expenditures have increased. When I was young, many farmers in Thanjavur would not send their children to school, they would also work in the field. Today, every family rightly has an aspiration to send their child, whether boy or girl, to school. With the collapse of the public sector, money is needed for private health care and education. The prices of fertilisers have gone up with cuts in subsidies. Fertiliser use efficiency is often poor. So there is increasing expenditure to meet growing needs, alongside diminishing income. The situation is worse for farmers in dry farming, un-irrigated areas, who often need to borrow money to survive.

We made a study in Delhi villages through the Extension Division of IARI around 1967-68, once the Green Revolution had started, to find out what the farmers would do with the extra money earned. The first priority was better housing, and the second priority was better education for their children. These are good motivations, but the services were not available. While at ICAR as DG, I gave funds to M.S. Randhawa who was the then Vice Chancellor of the Punjab Agricultural University, to set up a School of Rural Architecture in the university for designing rural houses with better sanitation, air circulation, a proper shed for the buffaloes, and so on. They did good work, and Randhawa also started a museum of Punjab's Social History of Agriculture. He was a man of vision, who saw agriculture not just as an income-earning activity for the farmers, but the soul of their culture and way of life. What I am trying to say is that when there is money in the hands of farmers, they try to use it to improve their quality of life. Some may consume alcohol, but this is not the majority. We should not stereotype them as having no aspirations or desire for an improved quality of life.

After I returned from Wisconsin in 1954, my first job was with N. Parthasarathy at the Central Rice Research Institute (CRRI), Cuttack, in a project that involved crossing the *indica* and *japonica* varieties of rice to enhance yields. Good varieties were developed such as ADT 27, released at the Aduthurai station in Tamil Nadu, though they didn't achieve the expected results. When I shifted to Indian Agriculture Research Institute (IARI), New Delhi, at the end of 1954, I suggested the need for research to develop a new plant architecture for wheat to the then Director, B.P. Pal, who himself was a wheat breeder. We experimented with a number of approaches, including radiation treatment for short and erect mutations (dwarfing), but they didn't work.

Meanwhile, we learnt from Dr Hitoshi Kihara, a well-known wheat scientist from Japan, that they had a dwarf variety of wheat called Norin 10, which we could request. The same variety had been taken to Washington State in the US by Dr Solomon, a scientist in General MacArthur's team, after the Allied victory in 1945, and given to Dr Orville Vogel at Washington State University. I wrote to Vogel. He was enthusiastic, but said that his varieties were of winter wheat, and suggested contacting Dr Norman Borlaug in Mexico, who was then working in a Rockefeller Foundation Programme, using the same dwarfing gene in a spring wheat background, more suitable to our conditions. I wrote to Borlaug. He had been experimenting with these seeds in Pakistan. So he went to Lahore, identified the varieties that were doing well, and provided us with some seeds. This history is recorded and therefore, I will not go into it here (Swaminathan, 2013).

Anyway, in October 1963, we started this work and I wrote a paper called 'Five Years of Dwarf Wheat' (1968) predicting that if everything was done according to the plan, then the *rabi* (crops sown in winter and harvested in spring) harvest in April 1968 would mark a new beginning in Indian agriculture. The first step was the setting up of National Demonstrations in the fields of small, resource-poor farmers, as I believed that if we could demonstrate a substantial increase in yields in their fields, the efficacy of these varieties would be proved; otherwise high yields can always be attributed to affluence. The member in charge of agriculture in the Planning Commission at that time, V.K.R.V. Rao, a very knowledgeable person and a great economist, who developed many institutions such as the Delhi School of Economics, didn't believe this. Neither did the officers in high positions; they felt the dwarf varieties would not be accepted by the farmers, as the straw (*bhusa*) might be less. They also didn't believe in going first to the small and resource-poor farmer, but preferred focusing attention on the better off, 'progressive' farmers. I asked them not to pre-judge, but ask the farmers and let them decide. They however didn't support my proposal, called the plan a waste of time, and no action was taken.

Fortunately, C. Subramaniam became Minister of Agriculture in 1964, after Lal Bahadur Shastri took over as Prime Minister. Shastri gave the famous slogan *'Jai Jawan, Jai Kisan'*, pointing to the defence forces and farmers as the two pillars of Independent India. With Shastri's support, and following Nehru's tradition and the belief that 'the future belongs to science and to those who make friendship with science', Subramaniam was a strong advocate of the use of science in all areas, not only agriculture.

With C. Subramaniam (then Governor, Maharastra), 1991.

Soon after taking over, he called all the senior scientists of IARI, about 20 of us, to Krishi Bhawan (Ministry of Agriculture's office) and went round the table asking each of us for our analysis. When it came to my turn, I spoke about the new technology—the seed varieties—available to us. If we applied it in the field on a large scale, we could break the yield stagnation, thereby helping to achieve the goal of the IADP programme. He asked what was coming in the way, and I said, I had wanted money, about ₹ 500 per hectare for 500 National Demonstrations, but the Ministry seemed to have some reservation and had not approved this. He asked his secretary to send him the file, and the very next day the clearance was issued for the National Demonstrations. In 1964 *rabi* season, we extended our trials all over India in order to identify those strains which were doing well in different locations and hence could be introduced in the National Demonstrations the following year.

We started the National Demonstrations in the fields of poor farmers, and it was a great success. The farmers got about five tonnes of wheat per hectare, instead of one. The message spread like wildfire. The rich came to the poor man's field and immediately took up the new varieties. What the extension agencies didn't appreciate was the tremendous extension value of demonstrating in a poor farmer's fields, whom they considered lacking in knowledge. There was a clamour for seeds, even the political leaders wanted seeds for their own farms. We told Subramanian that we should import some seeds in the short-term, what I called the 'purchase of time' operation, while we developed our own capacity for seed production.

This suggestion too ran into problems with the Planning Commission. V.K.R.V. Rao was somehow convinced that the dwarf varieties were not going to work and he was wary of enhancing allocations. They saw the wheat seed import as a waste of foreign exchange. I always believed in convincing the political administration not just by talking, but by demonstrating it in practice. I invited Prime Minister Shastri; he spent a couple of hours in the field and realised that we were close to a breakthrough. He wanted everything done to speed up and support our work. Despite going through a drought and

With Lal Bahadur Shastri in the wheat fields at IARI, 1965.

with limited foreign exchange reserves, he supported the import of 18,000 tonnes of seeds from Mexico.

Your maternal grandfather (S. Bhoothalingam) was the Finance Secretary at that time, and negotiated within the administration to get the funds cleared. His only condition was that the seeds should be delivered in time for the *rabi* sowing. We imported 18,000 tonnes of seeds from Mexico in 1966. Bhoothalingam wrote:

> An early and outstanding example of this approach made it possible for Dr M.S. Swaminathan to initiate effectively what came to be known later as the Green Revolution. We had to import the high-yielding varieties of wheat seed evolved by Dr Borlaug. The usual procedure would have been for the Ministry of Agriculture to make their demand. This would be followed by haggling, almost on the model of the Indian bazaar, and the final approval would have been for half the amount. In this

case, Dr Swaminathan explained to me that ₹ 5 crore would be necessary. I said, 'Certainly, if you assure me that it can be usefully spent for the purpose in view'.

I was astounded, therefore, when a few days later the Secretary, Agriculture, started the bargaining process by cutting the demand by half! Now when my officers suggested that I cut it down by a further half and I said that the whole amount would be a complete waste, they were delighted to find that I had become an orthodox finance man so quickly! I told them that Dr Swaminathan and the Agriculture Secretary were to see me the next day and that they should also join me. All of them were surprised by the kind of questions I asked because they were on entirely new lines; is the average cultivator likely to follow your advice? What is his growing season? When does the sowing start and what is the date by which it must end? They answered that the sowing season was roughly six weeks—November and the first half of December by the latest. I then said that the seeds must, therefore, be available to the farmer by at least the middle of October. As a result, it would have to be in Bombay by at least the beginning of October. In that case, what was the last date by which the seeds must actually be shipped from Mexico? I told them to look into all this and let me know. For the time being, I assumed it would be the first week of September.

Then I announced my decision:

You are authorised to make contracts for whatever quantity you like, with the overriding condition that the balance not shipped by 10 September will be cancelled. Whatever foreign exchange is actually spent on this contract is hereby authorised.

It would be obvious that without such conditions not an acre would have been sown that year. In the event, only one crore of rupees was actually spent, but practically all the seeds imported were sown in time (Bhoothalingam, 1993: 107-8).

I had also recommended that to get the yields we expected, we needed to provide 60 kg of nitrogen per hectare, for which the government should give a subsidy. The Planning Commission, however, recommended that instead of giving 60 kg per hectare, we should provide 30 kg per hectare and double the area under the new varieties. I strongly objected. If the input was halved to 30 kg per hectare, the yield increase would be nominal, rather than the quantum jump of 2-3 times that we expected. The larger the difference in yield, the greater would be the impact on the farmer. We needed to demonstrate what the plant was capable of yielding. While he could see the point, V.K.R.V. Rao never believed that such a quantum jump was possible. At the All India Wheat Workshop held at Jaipur in 1966, he even said that he would be more than happy if India ever produced 15 million tonnes of wheat. This was a major policy confrontation, as the bureaucrats had so far themselves decided what was good or bad for the farmers—the latter were never given a voice. Fortunately, Subramaniam was on our side.

In the meanwhile, we were making our own selections from the Mexican material, segregating material for varieties like *Kalyan Sona* and *Sonalika*, which had amber rather than red grains, the same dwarf plant height, and high yield potential. The demand for these seeds was very high; so alongside the imports, I started the Jounti Seed village in 1965 for the speedy production of seeds. In fact, Indira Gandhi, the then Prime Minister, inaugurated their seed processing plant in 1968, named Jawahar Jounti Seed Village after Nehru.

So we had a multi-pronged strategy—on one hand, there was a seed village approach and on the other, we imported seeds to save time. As a result, in 1968, we had a million hectares under the dwarf wheat from 4 hectares in 1963-64 and 40 hectares in 1964-65, and the wheat production went to a high of 17 million tonnes. V.K.R.V. Rao was kind enough to admit that he had never expected such a yield increase to happen in reality. I had predicted in 1963 that 1968 would be the starting point of a new chapter in Indian history and that really happened. There was a lot of opposition even at that time, a lack of faith in science as a prime mover of change, but the farmers were on our side and so was public policy, at least from 1965 to the late 1970s.

Control over Seeds: From Public Good to Commercial Research

NR: *As you have often mentioned, the Green Revolution has been critiqued by environmentalists on grounds of pollution, groundwater depletion, soil erosion and ecological damage, and economists for increasing inequality between regions and classes, especially discrimination against poor farmers. Activists and NGOs have also been critical, speaking largely of its ill-effects. The positive impacts seemed to have been forgotten.*

I recollect distinctly a village meeting in Jharkhand's Dumka District, listening to NGO speakers campaigning for seed sovereignty, asking farmers not to take or use any seed varieties from outside, not even those distributed at highly subsidised rates by the government to small and marginal farmers. They spoke against Monsanto, the big genetically modified (GM) seeds company, the Green Revolution and how soon the country would become a slave of US multinationals and corporates. Some of the speakers had come from Delhi and Kolkata, but the audience, mostly Santhal women and men, was local. A speaker mentioned how farmers in Bardhaman, a neighbouring district in West Bengal, were starving due to the high cost of production post-Green Revolution, and migrating in hordes to South India to work as agricultural labourers.

The next speaker was a woman from a nearby village. She spoke in Santali and her speech was translated by the NGO functionaries. She pointed out that she and hundreds of others from the district migrated to Bardhaman to work in the paddy fields as agricultural labour four times a year. While their working conditions were hard, they earned enough to meet their basic needs. She asked why the granaries of farmers in Bardhaman were always full, their children didn't go to sleep hungry, while what grew on her farm barely lasted a few weeks, despite the better natural endowment—water, soil and forest—in Jharkhand. The NGO functionaries silenced her and made her sit down.

The Hindu, on 27 May 2014, reported that the Punjab Chief Minister had approved subsidies to hybrid maize seeds produced by three companies—Monsanto, Pioneer and Shri Ram. Farmers' unions in Punjab have questioned this decision favouring multinational companies in terms of helping farmers in distress, as it would only destabilise the precarious ecosystem further. How far do you think that the unequal access to and control over high yielding varieties of seeds have contributed to inequality and farmer distress in recent times?

MSS: The term 'green revolution' was coined by William Gaud, the then Director of the US Agency for International Development (USAID), not by us; but it captured at that time the enthusiasm amongst the farmers, the scientists and the politicians. The breakthrough we had achieved was in wheat yields. There was some success in rice, but less so in maize, *jowar* and *bajra*. In the case of wheat and rice, the farmers could keep their own seed, but the others were hybrids which needed to be purchased each year. Just to clarify, while the seeds of a variety produced by Mendelian breeding can be retained by the farmers for use in future years, in a hybrid, the seed will segregate in the second generation (F2), leading to a decline in yield. So while hybrids do yield more, the seed has to be purchased every year, increasing the costs of production.

Sometimes science is confused with the organisation of production and distribution. Many of the criticisms at that time were not against the technology *per se*, but because of the institutions involved, such as the Rockefeller Foundation. As John D. Rockefeller was connected with the fertiliser industry, the Green Revolution was seen as a mechanism to sell American fertiliser. Similarly, since Borlaug was an American, there was even a charge that America was trying to push its technologies into India. Most of these apprehensions were ideological.

They didn't understand that Borlaug and others did not come on their own. We had first analysed why we should go for dwarf wheat and then approached him for seeds. It was not he who suggested us to grow dwarf wheat, we had to persuade him. He said he would like to come and see the growing conditions, as he had given some material to Pakistan. He and I travelled all over the wheat belt of North India in March 1963, and only after he was convinced, did we start working together. In fact, in a letter to me dated 10 November 1970, following the award of the Nobel Peace Prize, Borlaug wrote:

> The Green Revolution has been a team effort and much of the credit for its spectacular development must go to Indian officials, organizations, scientists and farmers. However, to

With Norman Borlaug.

> you, Dr Swaminathan, a great deal of the credit must go for first recognizing the potential value of the Mexican dwarfs. Had this not occurred it is quite possible that there would not have been a green revolution in Asia.

This year our farmers have produced 95 million tonnes of wheat; at the yield level of 1960, we would need 95 million hectares of land. But we are cultivating this on about 30 million hectares. As I emphasised in one of my lectures in 1966, the Green Revolution is both a land-saving and forest-saving agriculture. The pressure for enhanced crop production has meant a diversion of land from forests to agriculture, and a loss in our biodiversity. Forest area in India is now down to 18 per cent from 35 per cent in 1947.

The economists' critique was that the new seeds did not constitute an inclusive technology. Science is not a magic wand, science can only provide the options. It is up to the economists and policy makers to decide on what kind of support we should extend to the small farmers so as to enable them to take up the technology. The technologies are not resource-neutral, they are scale-neutral: they can be adopted by any farmer, who has access to seeds, to fertiliser and so on. Instead of analysing their constraints, if we simply say that a small farmer cannot avail of the technology, yes then they cannot do so. The key point about yields is that inputs are needed for output; the plant cannot produce out of nothing, it is not a magician. Science on its own cannot solve social problems or inequity; this needs the interaction between technology and public policy. Technologies can show how to improve the yield; only public policy will decide whether the yield is improved or not. If inputs are not available, or outputs are not priced properly, farmers will not adopt improved technologies. We need a fusion of scientific skill and political action to make progress.

But coming back to your query on the control of seeds, at that time the research programme was entirely in the domain of 'public good institutions' such as IARI and agricultural universities. As government institutions, their driving force was public good rather than profit, hence the agenda too was different from that of the private sector. The focus was on developing risk-minimising and risk-aversion technologies to insulate the poor farmer from unnecessary risks.

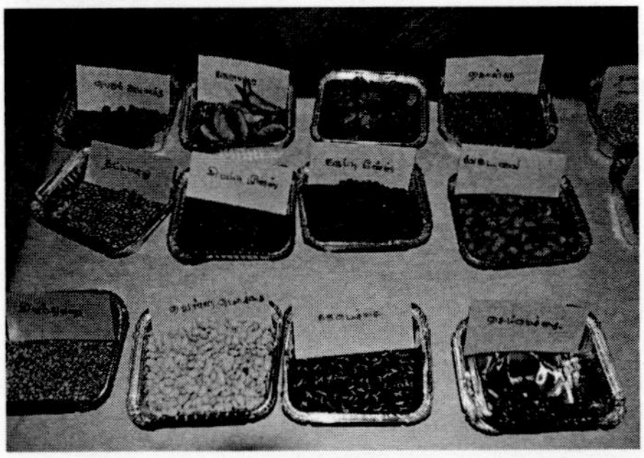

Seed varieties on display

Private companies promote hybrid seeds, as this means the farmer has to purchase it from the company each year, but a public good institution should develop varieties where a farmer can keep his own seeds. In Vidarbha, I believe so many suicides would not have taken place, but for the fact that the farmers had to buy costly seeds every year; and if the rains failed and so do the crops, then the money borrowed from money lenders at high interest rates are lost. If there was a high-yielding, pest-resistant variety where they could have kept their own seeds, things may not have been the same. I have been against the move to replace rice with hybrid rice, on a large scale, because rice is a plant where farmers keep their own seeds; why should we expose them to risk maximising technologies? Many varieties are as good as hybrids in yield potential.

Somehow today public good institutions seem to be imitating the private sector. For example, even with genetic modification, in 1990 when we started some work at the MSSRF, I chose to work on genes for sea water tolerance in the coastal mangroves as a preparation for sea level rise. This is not an area of interest to the private sector, which focuses mainly on food and cash crops for profit. Rather than imitating the private sector, there should be a clear agenda for public good research, an agenda for small farmers, which identifies the challenges they face and responds to it. This social and ethical dimension should be ingrained in public good research. Unfortunately, this is by and large missing today.

NR: *I think not only the research itself, but information about its use and application is also vitally important. For instance, there are indigenous varieties of seeds—high yielding varieties, hybrids, genetically modified seeds—it is not always clear what their relative costs and benefits are?*

MSS: I can give a stark example. James Watson and Francis Crick, who got the Nobel Prize in 1962 (along with Maurice Wilkins), were my contemporaries at Cambridge. I was at the Cambridge Plant Breeding Institute, and they were working in the Cavendish Laboratory. I used to take a course there on X-ray diffraction methods and so used to meet them as my peer PhD researchers. We would have a cup of tea occasionally in the cafeteria. Nobody expected that their finding of the DNA Double Helix structure would have such profound influence. In fact when they published their paper in *Nature* in 1953, their own claims were modest. It was only 30 years later, in the 1980s, that their discovery started having an impact. Untill then, it was more an era of Mendelian breeding. The main advantage of recombinant DNA technology is that you have access to the whole of the world's germplasm and can transfer genes across sexual and other barriers. It helps pick precise genetic characteristics rather than experimenting with many hundred of crosses. While developed at a university, the application of this technology has been monopolised by big companies, and once they monopolise it, they acquire patents to secure their IPR (intellectual property rights). So here is the issue around equity of access, which is lost when the private sector takes over what should be public good research.

In fact, once, probably in 1977, I met Margaret Thatcher at a reception hosted by the then British High Commissioner, John Thompson in Delhi. I was introduced to her as a Fellow of the Royal Society. She wanted to speak to me for a few minutes at the end. She said that while the British made the discoveries, the Americans made the money, and asked how this growing dichotomy between public good research in UK universities, and the practical application and monopolisation by multinational companies could be bridged. I replied that public good institutions should invest in translational research, the various intermediate steps required to convert research findings into practical applications, something that the American companies were adept at.

I think in the past, agriculture was not considered a fertile ground for private profit, as seeds were all under the control of farmers; even for improved varieties, they could keep their own seeds. But today companies are using biotechnologies to produce hybrid seeds, wherein farmers lose control and become dependent on the purchase of seeds from the market year after year. Companies therefore prefer hybrids to varieties. I think this trend has contributed to the distress of small farmers; they lose control and become entirely dependent on the market, not just the monsoons and nature. For small farmers, we need a combination of home-grown and market-purchased inputs.

Protection of Farmers' Rights: Conserver, Breeder and Cultivator

NR: *Over the last two decades, many NGOs have started promoting organic and traditional agriculture, both in protest of the multinational control over seeds and to ensure seed sovereignty. You retired from the Government of India in 1981, yet your concern for equity and farmers' rights has remained alive. Can you tell me a little about how you have maintained and expressed this concern?*

MSS: Equity in access is important. That is why even when I designed the National Demonstrations, I insisted this should take place in the small farmers' fields. I don't know if this is still the case. Earlier when research was more in the public domain, the issue of IPR was not so important, as the purpose of research was to make it inclusive and accessible, rather than exclusive. With commercialisation and patenting by companies, it has become important for public good institutions like IARI as well as agricultural universities to engage with some level of defensive patenting, so that the ideas and technologies meant for the public good are not misappropriated for private profit. Even in MSSRF, there are some varieties which have genes from the mangrove *Avicennia marina* for salt water tolerance. They have not been approved for release because of the ban on field testing of GM seeds of food crops. However, in order to ensure that the work is not taken over by commercial bodies, we have taken a defensive patent on this. When I was Chairperson of MSSRF, I got a resolution from the Board of Trustees that these defensive patents should be made available to farmers through processes of participatory breeding, that is, farmers can cross the new variety with the gene for salt tolerance with their own varieties. We do the pre-breeding, or developing a gene for a particular quality; this can then be combined with participatory breeding.

In fact, there is another variety with us which is highly drought-tolerant, drawing this quality from *Prosopis juliflora*. In all dry farming areas like Pudukottai and Ramanathapuram districts of Tamil Nadu, farmers could be trained to use this gene to develop locally adapted varieties. This would ensure inclusive access to technology. We have to develop new and innovative approaches to help farmers develop their own varieties with our new material, which unfortunately institutions such as the agricultural universities are not doing today. If we adopt a pre-cum-participatory breeding approach, we can combine genetic diversity with genetic efficiency and equity.

When I was at IRRI, I once visited the rice terraces of Mt Banaue in the Philippines with an American anthropologist, Dr Harold Conklin. He asked me if I wanted to meet the world's best plant breeder? I said yes certainly, and he took to me to meet a young Ifugao lady. She was an excellent breeder. She had what he called 'a seeing eye and understanding heart', an ability to identify the winners. We shouldn't underestimate the capacity of local people for breeding, what I call "every farmer a scientist."

This was my idea behind the seed villages we promote in MSSRF: to enable farmers as seed breeders and producers to benefit from their skill, and to have knowledge-intensive rather than capital or chemical-intensive agriculture. We cannot give them land, only the government can, but we can give them new skills which are marketable and can enhance their earnings, while also reducing drudgery of work. Following the success of Jounti Seed Village in the 1960s, we had

UPOV has not recognised the Indian legislation because they think that farmers' rights and breeders' rights should not be confused. My argument has been that without the farmer, there would be no need for breeders, so their rights should be mutually reinforcing rather than remaining antagonistic. The problem is one of unequal power relations. Those with degrees, and who have been in scientific laboratories, think they know everything, but the fact remains that farmers have been brought up in the laboratory of life where they learn by experience. Many scientific discoveries have their roots in traditional knowledge.

Take, for example, medicinal plants. Nature only sees it as a plant; it is somebody's knowledge, usually that of local communities, that has found a medicinal property in a particular plant. Scientists use this knowledge, but do not acknowledge it. 'Unlearn and learn' must be our philosophy for all young researchers. They should try to respect knowledge from wherever it comes, whether it is from the home, the field or the laboratory. This requires an attitudinal change, learning to respect each other, accepting the farmer as an equal. Changing social relations and attitudes I think is the bigger challenge than the scientific one.

4

Integrated Planning and Management of Resources

Intellectual Influences

NR: *As a social scientist, the interconnections between different domains of life—the economic and the social—are obvious to me; that people live within communities and societies, and 'give and take' is both expected and practised. Social and human relationships of love, care and respect are often more valued than material wealth. Yet, as you have yourself noted, most scientists seem to work in compartments, as do bureaucracies. The ultimate goal of producing food is to ensure adequate consumption and nutrition, even for the poorest; yet fragmentation in terms of the conceptualisation of social relations and natural resources as distinct rather than interconnected, and the resulting lack of coordination amongst delivery systems, have made this goal difficult to achieve. What have been the influences on your own thinking, and how have you been able to sustain your approach, in an increasingly fragmented and divided polity and society?*

MSS: There is a sea of change in intellectual traditions and influences as compared to that 70 years ago, but we also seem to be coming a full circle now. I think the culture of education is probably responsible for the change. In the past, education was more holistic, looking at problems in their totality. Prof J.B.S. Haldane, the brilliant geneticist and mathematician, whose work established the unification of Mendelian genetics and Darwinian evolution by natural selection, moved to India in the 1950s and later settled down at Bhubaneswar. I recall Haldane coming to Indian Agriculture Research Institute (IARI) and we took him round the farm. He commented on the great difference he saw between our farm and the farmer's farm. In the latter, he saw mixed cropping and multiple cropping, crop rotation, and crop-livestock integrated farming. In the research institute, he found scientists each working on a separate problem, somebody working on wheat, somebody on pests. Farmers' farming is centred on natural resources, while scientists often work with a commodity-centred approach. Haldane observed a mismatch between what farmers were doing and what scientists were doing. Unless the two came together in terms of understanding the ecosystem as a whole, it would be difficult to make progress.

He was right, as in the initial years after Independence, we did have a crop-centric, animal-centric approach, so fodder crops became the responsibility of the Agriculture Department, while animal care was with the Animal Husbandry Department. The focus of the latter was more on animal health management, rather than nutrition, breeding, processing, marketing and pricing. While disease management is important, it is not enough. This was one of the reasons why milk production in India was stagnating at 20 million tonnes for a long time, although we had more than 400 million buffaloes, cows, sheep and goats. It was only when Kurien broke this kind of compartmentalisation and brought together nutrition, health care, breeding, and the whole question of processing and marketing through the cooperatives, that milk production went up. Today we are the world's top producer of milk, producing more than 135 million tonnes per year. This shows the power of synergy, of putting all the pieces together in a 'systems' approach.

We realised that the two cultures had got separated—the research culture and the farmers' culture. The two had to meet and interact, and that is what we tried through the National Demonstrations, as well as through the lab-to-land and the land-to-lab programmes. Scientists started understanding why farmers do certain things, for example, mixed cropping. When I first travelled to Punjab, I noticed that farmers always grew chickpea (*chana*), wheat, barley and mustard in small amounts; if one crop failed, there would be others. Rather than a profit-maximising agronomy, it is risk-distribution agronomy. People like Haldane brought to our attention quite early that unless scientists became more natural resource management-centred, looking at what the farmers have in terms of land, water and other facilities available, it would be impossible to understand their requirements or support them in a meaningful manner.

An even earlier influence was F.L. Brayne, who wrote a book called *Socrates in an Indian Village*. He lived near Norwich, and I had an opportunity to stay with him one Christmas, when I was a student at Cambridge. Brayne had been the Commissioner of Punjab and insisted on looking at the problems of rural India and of agriculture holistically. He focused on the consolidation of land holdings, on land levelling, water management, rural roads, storage and electricity. Perhaps this was a reason why Punjab benefitted from the Green Revolution much earlier than other regions, as a supportive agrarian and land management structure was already in place. He was also critical of his own British colleagues at that time. Another exception was Albert Howard, the Director of the Pusa Institute established in Bihar in 1905. He was both a wheat breeder and an organic farmer.

Even among Indian scientists, people like K. Ramaiah and B.P. Pal were systems' people, looking at the problem in its totality. While leading the *indica-japonica* hybridisation programme, Ramaiah was clear that we needed to pay attention to water management, soil fertility management, nutrient management, and ensure varietal diversity, because varietal homogeneity enhances genetic vulnerability to pests and diseases.

Borlaug was more a commodity-centred person since he wanted to solve the food problem as quickly as possible. His mandate was wheat, his institute (International Maize and Wheat Imptovement Center; CIMMYT) was working on wheat and maize. He worked with single-minded devotion on wheat improvement, including pest and disease control in wheat. People like Borlaug showed that wheat production can be increased enormously by changing the plant architecture. Yet I had realised that some synergy was needed and also interaction with the farmers. So when the new varieties came from Borlaug, I started the pan-IARI project. I had a meeting with all the Departmental Heads, of plant pathology, agronomy, soil science, extension, entomology, economics and statistics, and we charted out a common strategy. For example, the late S. Pradhan, Head of Division of Entomology, played a very important role even beyond the field of entomology. Being a man from the field, he understood the problems of farmers in their totality, as did Daroga Singh, the Head of the Agricultural Statistics Division. They developed a storage facility called the Pusa Bin, as well as a *neem* decoction that could be sprayed on plants as an insect repellent against locusts and other pests. These methods were based on the experience of farmers and used locally available material. Traditional knowledge and modern science were blended; unfortunately this approach is missing today. If you are a biotechnologist, you just worship biotechnology and genetic modification, rather than finding solutions through Mendelian breeding, molecular breeding or a blend of the two.

When you asked about intellectual and cultural traditions, there are at least three. One is building from where you are, learning from the past, from traditional wisdom, the traditional knowledge and the ecological prudence of local communities. Secondly, the farming system needs to be seen in its totality—land, water and soil. Haldane's praise of the farmers' culture was based on what he saw as an optimisation of the natural resources available to them. The third is recognition that for farmers, agriculture is a way of life, their main subsistence; hence rather than maximising profits, they seek to reduce risk.

Some years ago, I heard Prince Charles deliver the Albert Howard lecture on the value of organic farming. I feel that dividing farming into organic and chemical is again a narrow approach. Organic farming doesn't mean that you don't use pesticides, for instance, but that these can be organic pesticides such as *neem*. When the pressure of population increases and we want to produce more from less land, the plant requires more nutrition. I always give the example of the child requiring Vitamin C for a running nose. You can tell a child to take six oranges or a 100 mg tablet. For a poor child, the only possibility is the tablet as six oranges would be too costly. So today, we need a cafeteria approach, making available a mix of technologies which are relevant to farmers in different conditions. Ecological stability should however remain the bottom line.

NR: *Are some of these ideas being recognised by political leaders?*

MSS: Today, we are again placing emphasis on natural resources management-centred farming, instead of a commodity-centred approach. This is fundamental for achieving what I call an 'evergreen revolution', which is, increasing production in perpetuity.

I had invited the American Ambassador Kenneth Marsh and his wife to the release of my book *From Green to Evergreen Revolution* at the residence of the then Prime Minister Manmohan Singh on 28 September 2010. Marsh liked the idea very much, and asked if he could have two copies of the book—one for President Obama, who was scheduled to visit India later in the year. The President mentioned the need for an 'evergreen revolution' in his address to the Indian Parliament on 8 November 2010. He noted:

> Together, we can strengthen agriculture. Cooperation between Indian and American researchers and scientists sparked the Green Revolution. Today, India is a leader in using technology to empower farmers, like those I met yesterday who get free updates on market and weather conditions on their cell phones. And the United States is a leader in agricultural productivity and research. Now, as farmers and rural areas face the effects of climate change and drought, we'll work together to spark a second, more sustainable Evergreen Revolution (*http://www.whitehouse.gov/the-press-office/2010/11/08/remarks-president-joint-session-indian-parliament-new-delhi-india*).

I got several emails from American scientists and friends in the US saying they were very happy that he had adopted this approach. Nevertheless, in India, little has been done so far to make this a reality.

Learning from the Field: Water, Grain, Seed and Gene Banks

NR: *Some years ago, I read the report of John Augustus Voelcker, a consultant chemist to the Royal Agricultural Society of England. In 1889, the Imperial Government brought him to India with the mandate of suggesting measures to improve Indian agriculture. Voelcker toured the length and breadth of the country for about 10 months. After talking about the great diversity of both agriculture and the people, he went on to say* *that the average Indian farmer was as good as the average British farmer, and in fact, often superior. He praised the integrated system of farming, crop rotation and mixing as well as animal husbandry prevalent in India. While he advocated the use of science, he recommended that the scientists work in close collaboration with the farmers and constantly keep in mind the changing field realities. So in that sense it is clear that even in those years, there was a dual approach, with one school advocating holism and the other focussing on individual aspects of agriculture. The latter seems to have been historically stronger, perhaps because there was no one to actively demonstrate a holistic approach or ways it could be actualised in the field. How did you demonstrate that it could be done?*

MSS: I first proposed the idea of the four Cs—conservation, cultivation, commerce and consumption—as the plank for MS Swaminathan Research Foundation's (MSSRF's) Wayanad Centre, and I must say they have taken this up quite seriously. What does it mean really? The major lesson is that it recognises the multiple roles of farmers not only as cultivators, conservers and breeders, but also as consumers.

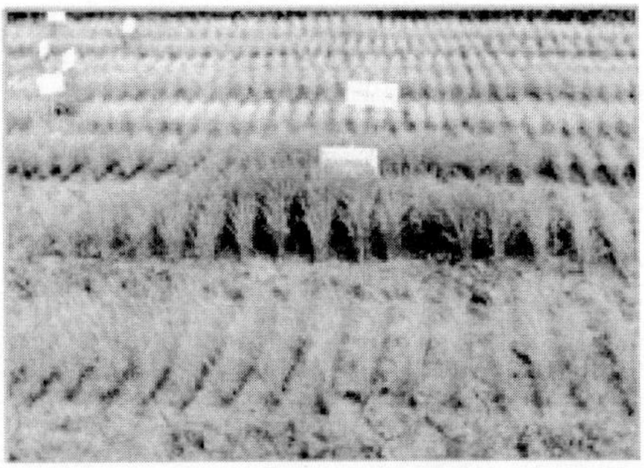

In situ conservation.

Conservation here means *in situ*, on-farm conservation, where there is also a process of evolution alongside preservation. Other ways of conservation include cryogenic preservation (keeping the material in freezers). Conservation works itself through two practices—a seed bank and a gene bank. While genes are conserved *in situ*, seed varieties from the fields are kept in seed banks. This identifies the three main axes of cultivation, the other two being soil and water, without which cultivation itself will not be possible.

We cannot make agriculture secure without water security, and this cannot be ensured in a purely monsoon-based agriculture. This is why in my recent article, 'Managing the Monsoon' (*The Hindu*, 2 May

Seed Bank, Koraput.

2014), I have said that we must make water harvesting mandatory at all levels—in the household, farms and factories. This should become a habit, as our rainfall is not only deficient in parts, but also skewed in its distribution. If you get heavy rains for just two days, the monsoon budget may be fulfilled, but this will do more damage than good. Meghalaya in general and Cherapunji in particular (now called Sohra) for instance, have the highest rainfall in the country. But they were not storing it and have faced water shortage between March and May.

Only as recently as 2009, the Department of Science and Technology launched a programme called WAR (Winning, Augmentation and Renovation) for Water as a win-win method of water harvesting through augmentation of supplies, and renovation of tanks and wells (*http://dst.gov.in/scientific-programme/plan-document.pdf*). Farmers are asked to make a farm pond (*jal kund*) and store the water. This has become a popular movement as it addresses a location-specific, ecosystem-specific need. In fact the Mahatma Gandhi National Rural Employment Guarantee Scheme (MGNREGS) based on

Conserving rain water: A farm pond.

the National Rural Employment Guarantee Act (NREGA)[1] can be used for this purpose, for rejuvenation, maintaining and creating structures for harvesting rain water. We got the National Water Award for 2012 for our work in Koraput—it was nothing extraordinary but revival of a few old ponds. But this enabled the local people to grow pulses, which are of high value and require less of water.

The grain bank is a place to safely store the grains post-harvest. This was common in tribal areas during the colonial period because if the rains failed, this was the method through which communities could support each other during phases of starvation and death. It was meant to ensure local food security. Unfortunately, in recent years, little attention has been paid to post-harvest processing and storage,

1. Passed in 2005, NREGA provides for the enhancement of livelihood security of the households in rural areas of the country by providing at least 100 days of guaranteed wage employment in every financial year to every household whose adult members volunteer to do unskilled manual work (*http://nrega.nic.in/netnrega/home.aspx*).

Different forms of grain storage.

leading to grains rotting in state warehouses. The idea of commerce is often ignored, but farmers need marketable surplus to generate cash income for their multiple needs. Attention to all these components is necessary—ensuring conservation, sustainable cultivation, alongside food security and sufficient incomes for meeting other needs. Finally, the farmer is also a consumer, unless there is demand for a particular grain or product, it will not be produced; hence we find, for instance, a decline in the production of local grains like millets.

We have demonstrated the linkages between agronomy, water, climate, the protection of genetic diversity and ways to integrate these components in order to enhance the opportunities for local people so as to have a plan from end-to-end for their farm, starting with conservation of the natural resource base, to cultivation that is sustainable in its use of resources, and finally consumption of their local grains—this will help to conserve the food traditions.

While the government has 50-60 million tonnes of food grains, almost one-fourth of the population is undernourished. Amartya Sen spoke of inequities in distribution, but alongside this, consumption is important, as calorie deprivation arises from inadequate consumption, which in turn is linked to the lack of purchasing power, lack of skilled jobs and so on. One question has always troubled me: what is the use of producing more, securing the first or second rank in the world, when a large part of the population remains malnourished? Why are we saving the mangroves, if it is not to protect the future of children who depend on the mangrove ecosystems? The ultimate purpose of producing more is to improve both the purchasing power and the consumption capacity of the poorest. Therefore, while trying to enhance production, we should not forget those for whom we are producing. When politicians talk of food self-sufficiency, I have always pointed out that the current levels of purchasing power are inadequate for nutrition security. Gandhiji said at Noakhali, "There are people in the world so hungry, that God cannot appear to them except in the form of bread."

The National Food Security Act 2013, and the expansion of the food basket have created an opportunity to stabilise and expand cultivation of some of the crops that might otherwise be 'lost'. There is also an opportunity to expand community-owned and managed storage facilities. But the upscaling of the approach depends upon support from the government and local agricultural universities. Unfortunately, they have not yet started thinking about managing natural resources in a holistic manner, but continue teaching each element as a distinct discipline.

Thinking Multi-dimensionally: Pro-Nature, Pro-Poor and Pro-Women

NR: *Something which I have admired and learnt from you is your ability to think multi-dimensionally, temporally, spatially and across different domains of life. For instance, you are easily able to connect the past, present and future, learning lessons from the past as we confront future challenges; and to find the links from the local to the global, from practice to policy, from people, in particular women and the poor, to environmental, climate and scientific concerns, from production to distribution and consumption. Such a depth and breadth of vision is uncommon to find. Here I really want to understand how you developed this vision, reflected now in the mandate of MSSRF, what were the key moments, experiences, the influences that contributed towards it?*

MSS: I call these the three pillars of sustainable human advancement. The first stares you in the face, the loss of biodiversity, the loss of good soil, the over-exploitation of ground water, as human-induced climate change. I have seen this myself. When I joined the Coimbatore Agriculture College in 1944, the water-table was about 20-25 metres below the ground, now it is 900 metres below. The Stockholm Conference on human environment in 1972 was a wake-up call; of course, Indira Gandhi made a famous statement there that one cannot talk about the environment without taking into account the needs of the poor. With industrialisation, and more and more emphasis on economic growth, our natural resources are not really taken into account. Between 1984 and 1990, when I was President of the International Union for Conservation of Nature and Natural Resources (IUCN), and visited many areas, I saw the enormous loss of biodiversity, particularly coastal mangroves being cut down for aquaculture ponds. I started giving serious thought to sustainable agriculture, and identified the three dimensions—environment friendliness, the social dimensions and of course economic sustainability.

I chose pro-nature as the first point because whatever we do must be sustainable over a period of time; it should ensure inter-generational equity. If we destroy the environment today, what about the future generations who have to live in the same land? The choice of pro-nature was conditioned by the unsustainable development practices around us, all over the world, not only in India. I knew when I started MSSRF that I had to try and operationalise the concept of 'evergreen revolution'. In 2015, the UN wants to launch the Sustainable Development Decade, as the consequences of environmental depletion and genetic erosion are becoming clear.

However, we can't think of the environment without the people who inhabit it. Inequality today is increasing and in turn leading to violence. Long ago, the Roman philosopher Seneca, the Younger (4th century BC-65 AD) said, "A hungry person listens not to reason, nor cares for justice, nor is bent by any prayers. He wants food today." In terms of social sustainability, I then identified two elements gender and poverty. Working in agriculture, when going round the villages, I could see the conditions of the landless labourers. There was no NREGS, no work for many people, and they were starving. They had to migrate to cities and urban areas, leaving behind the women to manage whatever little land or resources they may have. At the same time, women faced social discrimination and violence. I have seen the women working very hard in Haryana and Punjab, but their contributions were completely unrecognised and unrewarded. These are the social realities in our country.

MSSRF was not designed to be a centre for social transformation *per se*; rather the goal was to use science and technology to trigger social change. However, we had to be sensitive to the needs of different groups of people. When we started the bio-villages in Puducherry, we were fortunate to have a very sensitive person, Shyamasundaran Nair, to help convert the concept into action. The first step was to clarify the concept of a bio-village and identify the criteria that would

the focus on discrete activities versus a more holistic approach to farming. Can you tell me a little more about the changes and learning over time?

MSS: The past, present and future is a continuum; we can see this in the way technology has developed. We have to learn not only from past knowledge, recognise and reward it, but also learn from the mistakes that have been made, identify elements that are not desirable and so on. At MSSRF, I wanted to take into account the knowledge of the past; that is why I laid emphasis on the selection of tribal areas as our field sites. In my work with FAO on the Globally Important Agriculture Heritage Sites, I encouraged them to recognise certain areas, such as Kuttanad, where farmers have developed their own methods for below sea-level farming, as agricultural heritage sites. We talk about climate change and the melting of ice, but these farmers have adapted to the consequences of sea level rise, and we need to acknowledge and be guided by this in terms of our future practices.

When we convert our pro-nature, pro-poor and pro-women mandate into action, it translates into the adoption of eco-technologies. This, for me, includes the five Es: ecological sustainability, economic viability, (social) equity, employment generation and (renewable) energy. But of course the activities would need to change over time, as the context changes. For instance, the needs today are very different in Puducherry compared to that 25 years ago, when we started the bio-village programme. The whole region has been industrialised and thus, we need to adapt and respond to these changes. Unfortunately, many of the people in MSSRF today lack a sense of the past, of why the Foundation was set up, its ethical and intellectual roots and vision. They just start repeating what they already know, the same activities over and over again; this was however never the purpose—it was always to identify critical gaps in knowledge and fill them. It is more important to understand the core concepts as the specific activities can change.

From the Local to the Global

NR: *Being aware of changing contexts and responding to them can be quite challenging as it means being up-to-date with changes in both the micro-context and the macro-policy domain, be it at national or global level.*

How have you been able to keep pace and engage with the multiple levels of research, policy and practice?

MSS: Within science too, there are many different views: from 'small is beautiful' to the globalisation of knowledge. What I have learnt is that it is not science *per se*, but its control and application, and the power relations therein that lead to these polarised views. It is not that one or the other is good or bad. When I went to Holland in 1949 and then to Cambridge, my own research depended upon a number of potato species collected from the days of Vavilov, the famous Russian geneticist, from different parts of Latin America and the Andean region. Plants have moved across the world from a long time: maize may have originated in South America but became a very important food crop in Africa. Similarly, potato moved from the Andean region to Europe and India. The famous potato famine of Ireland was largely because a single strain of potato had been grown in large areas; so when this was affected by late blight, the entire crop was destroyed and many people died. If the concept of exchanging plant material and research data which is mutually beneficial had existed, a number of deaths could have been avoided. I realised early in my scientific career that we need purposeful international collaboration on a win-win basis.

When I came to Delhi and occupied positions in IARI and then Indian Council of Agricultural Research (ICAR), it was equally clear that we should draw upon the global pool of knowledge, if we want to 'purchase time'. We could have started work on mutation breeding ourselves, but when this knowledge was already available, why should we waste time, rather than collaborating with Japan, Mexico, Sweden and so on? The partnership with Borlaug was particularly productive because he was not only a wheat breeder but a great humanist; he transferred some of his enthusiasm for larger purposes too, such as eradication of hunger, besides increasing wheat production.

So when in 1971, there was a proposal from the World Bank, UNDP and FAO to set up a Consultative Group on International Agriculture Research (CGIAR), as DG, ICAR, I gave my full support. I had already seen the work of IRRI (International Rice Research

Institute, Philippines), CIMMYT, Mexico, IITA (International Institute of Tropical Agriculture, Nigeria) and CIAT (International Centre for Tropical Agriculture, Colombia). These were the four institutions originally set up by the Rockefeller and Ford Foundations; IRRI was the first one in 1960 with a focus on rice. The basic idea of these institutions was to develop a critical mass of inter-disciplinary effort, lacking within national systems. I have seen the impact of such a critical mass of inter-disciplinary effort in my own work at IARI in the case of wheat. We brought together a team of people from entomology, microbiology, agronomy, soil science, economics and extension, and the result was a doubling of wheat production in a short period of time and the discontinuation of PL480 imports.

NR: *Your engagement with Borlaug and CIMMYT dates back to the early 1960s. Could you give me some examples of your involvement in key global research and policy arenas prior to the 1980s?*

MSS: The CGIAR appointed a Technical Advisory Committee (TAC), chaired by a wonderful person, Sir John Crawford, who was the then Chancellor of the Australian National University at Canberra. I was elected as Vice Chairman; there were 10 others including the President of the Rockefeller Foundation. This forum gave me enormous opportunity to promote international collaboration on a win-win base, because it was the charter of CGIAR to work for the global public good.

First, was the establishment of the International Crops Research Institute for the Semi-Arid Tropics (ICRISAT) in Hyderabad in 1972. We had been working on sorghum and millets but their yield was low, they were susceptible to drought, and clearly we required a strong inter-disciplinary approach to make a breakthrough in these crops. Breeding alone was not enough. ICRISAT's aim was not merely improvement of sorghum and millets, but also chickpea, pigeon pea, other pulses, as well as groundnut.

The second proposal I put forward to the TAC was in 1974. When I was in the Botany division of IARI, my own Professor, Harbhajan Singh, a very fine man, was collecting plants from various places and wanted to develop a National Bureau of Plant Genetic Resources (NBPGR), which was finally established in 1974, when I was DG,

ICAR. I had wanted to organise similar bodies for animal, fish and forest genetic resources, but the then Planning Commission Chairman asked us to first start with the NBPGR. It is doing well in the cryogenic preservation (like the Svalbard Gene Vault) of several million samples of Indian varieties. At that time, I told Sir John Crawford that we must have an International Board of Plant Genetic Resources (IBPGR).[2] He had some doubts on whether such a board could lie in the purview of the CGIAR. I had wanted the Board of Trustees of IBPGR to be drawn from all the Vavilovian centres of origin of crop plants, to save whatever is remaining in the planet, because genetic erosion is strong. The proposal was finally approved, as I was also able to convince the then DG of FAO that without preserving germplasm, future work on crop plants and their improvement would become a problem.

Global effort can help in at least two ways. One is to assemble genetic materials from all over the world, conserve them and use them sustainably. The second is to promote an end-to-end approach to food security, often lacking in national systems.

NR: *Today we find that the global and national systems may be in competition with each other rather than collaborating on the basis of mutual respect. What do you feel about this?*

MSS: The question of the relationship between the international centres—the global public good system and the National Agricultural Research Systems (NARS)—is an important one. My conviction is that a well-organised national agriculture system which has strong capability can benefit more from the international system, because you know what you want from them, rather than just testing materials that they provide. We could collaborate on an equal footing with Borlaug and CIMMYT because we knew exactly what we wanted. Unfortunately today, this relationship is changing. The national systems are being eroded rather than strengthened. At the same time, the international centres are opening their own campuses and substations, rather than collaborating with national institutions. Salaries are higher in the international centres; so many scientists

2. IBPGR is now known as Bioversity International.

today are leaving the national system to join such organisations. This is not a healthy trend.

One of the issues I faced when I was DG of IRRI (1982-1988) was the salary differentials between the international and national scientists. Ninety per cent of the staff were local, and received their salaries in the local currency. I recall in my first year at IRRI, the Marcos regime was weakening. The Indian rupee and Philippine peso were the same, about 7-8 pesos or rupees per US dollar. Within a year, the value of the peso fell and became 20 pesos per dollar. Naturally, the local staff felt that the expatriates were earning two to three times more than them and resented this, though they didn't complain or say anything to me. I asked the Chief Finance Officer, Paul Cooper, how much we had gained as a result of devaluation. He gave me a figure. I decided to distribute this equally amongst all the Filipino staff at Christmas time, along with a food basket. That completely changed their attitude towards me. Strangely enough, the higher paid Filipino staff came to me and asked why I had distributed equally across the board, to the scientists and labourers, rather than distributing the surplus as a proportion of the salary. I heard them and said, "Let me tell you one thing, you are all Christians. I am not, I am a Hindu, but I thought that according to Christianity, Christmas is the time to share your blessings." This message spread very fast, that Swaminathan says we must be Christian in our lives and values! The other thing I did for the local staff was to give them perquisites such as loans for the purchase of cars, housing, etc. There are problems in the management of such international centres too, and it requires humanism to deal with the problems. This idea that our work should be for humanity was documented in the book *IRRI-Philippines: 50 Years of Progress Fighting Poverty and Hunger,* in its description of what they call the 'Swaminathan Era'.

I tried to build partnerships with local institutions and do micro-level, location-specific research, relevant to the host country and population. In fact, I helped set up the Philippines Rice Research Institute when I was DG of IRRI. Another change I made was to reach out for the first time to all the agriculture universities of Asia. Therefore, although the global can enrich the regional and national, a

with markets, NGOs (non-governmental organisations), and most importantly, the education system should also give the right signals. I feel that agricultural education in the agricultural universities should be called 'education for agriculture' because these two are different things. Agricultural education includes areas like agronomy, botany, zoology and plant pathology. But education for agriculture starts with the human being, the farmers and their families.

In fact, as early as 1965, when the Indian Education Commission (1964-1966), under the Chairmanship of Prof D.S. Kothari, popularly known as the Kothari Commission, was finalising its report, we (B.P. Pal and I) requested them to title the agricultural chapter as 'education for agriculture', and not 'agricultural education'. Education for agriculture would start with the basic realities of rural life, with issues of differential access to knowledge and technology for different groups of farmers—small and large, men and women. As I mentioned earlier, people like Brayne and Haldane looked at the totality of rural life. Unfortunately, I have not been able to change the system of agricultural education in our country. In fact, agriculture universities have now fragmented further into agriculture, horticulture, fisheries, veterinary science and so on.

The idea of the agriculture universities had originated from the Land Grant Colleges set up in the United States (US) by Abraham Lincoln over 150 years ago. They viewed agriculture in a holistic way. Nehru had been to the US and was impressed by the Land Grant institutions, so he came to an agreement with the US to help set up similar institutions in India. The first agricultural university in India was set up in Pantnagar, now in Uttarakhand, in 1960, with support from the University of Illinois. Currently there are 62 agriculture universities in the country. In the Union Budget for 2014-15, there is provision for four more.

In the original model, the agricultural university was given considerable land for two purposes—first, to earn some money for their own recurring expenditure from the farm, and secondly, to provide opportunities for students to do more practical work so as to gain experience in the laboratories as well as in the field. In fact, in the early years, Pantnagar even gave a little venture capital fund to groups of students to cultivate a piece of land, and asked them to keep any profit they were able to make. This was not only an incentive, particularly to resource-poor students, but also provided good training in the economics of farming.

Prior to Independence, when he was District Collector of Kurnool, your grandfather (S. Bhoothalingam) noted the immense knowledge of the village *karnams*. There was a system called *Annavari* (16 annas to a rupee). Whenever there was a drought or flood, the local *karnam* would estimate the loss in terms of *annas*. Relief measures would be related to the estimated loss; so if there was a four *anna* crop, that is, 75 per cent loss, then that percentage of loans and expenses would be set off. The system worked perfectly, as the *karnams* were able to predict the crop loss quite exactly because they were trained to observe and listen. When we talk about traditional wisdom and modern knowledge, I believe some of the traditional administrative practices like *Annavari* also need to be carefully examined, as they helped build close relationships between the administrative officers and the farmers. Today this relationship doesn't exist, so if the crop fails, the people have no option but to migrate for work. There is no safety measures, like the famine codes during British times, which laid out a set of action points to be followed in different scenarios. The power of observing, of listening to what people say, of understanding rural realities, is missing. Instead, whenever a natural calamity occurs, a team is sent from Delhi to recommend the support needed!

The same is the case with the National Extension Service. I was horrified to find, soon after I joined Indian Agriculture Research Institute (IARI) in the 1950s, that information on the 'package of practices' was printed centrally in Delhi and distributed all over India. I can understand developing a package of practices for a particular agro-ecosystem, but making one for the whole country is senseless. Part of the reason that the package programme was not working was the lack of an appropriate variety, but the other element was the lack of sensitivity towards diverse contexts. The practices need to be developed locally in a participatory manner in order to be most effective, not isolated from the rural reality. With the privatisation of research, and large institutions located in metros rather than in local contexts (like the Indian Council of Agricultural Research [ICAR] institutions), the distance from the field is only increasing, and locale-specific research is on the decline. It is only NGOs who now engage in participatory research, but out of necessity, and their work is small-scale in nature.

NR: *My mother, Mina Swaminathan, would often listen to our conversations. Rarely did she speak up, only when she felt very strongly about something. This was one such occasion.*

Mina: One of the problems in implementing the MS Swaminathan Research Foundation (MSSRF) mandate has been inadequate political and social consciousness amongst the scientists. I am not referring to any affiliation to political parties, but rather understanding the ways in which political solutions have been found for social problems globally, whether through communism or capitalism. They are not aware of caste, class and gender and how they intersect to play out in everyday life; also the degree to which their own attitudes internalise their class or caste position. Once you become self-aware, then it is possible to find ways to move ahead. In a way, young people today lack this wider sensitisation and exposure while growing up; they should get it through their education. Unfortunately, in agricultural universities, they miss out on learning about the larger world, and reading widely about global developments.

The same applies to public good institutions like ICAR. They tend to live in a limited world. They don't see how the everyday problems that people face, like rising petrol or kerosene prices, might affect what they are working on and the technologies they are promoting. Agriculture needs to be located in a broader context. When Appa started talking about climate change and sea level rise 25 years ago, not many had thought about it in the developing world; now it has become the fashion. Related to this closed working style is also a disciplinary divide. If scientists could work across disciplines, surely new insights will be generated.

Learning Strategies

NR: *You are right, but wouldn't the ability to work across disciplines require not only an open mind but multiple learning and sharing strategies?*

MSS: If we truly recognise and accept the contributions of the different actors in agriculture, then I would say we should give equal emphasis to four different kinds of learning strategies: lab-to-lab, lab-to-land, land-to-land and land-to-lab. While we have experimented with all four strategies, the first three are more institutionalised; the last much more challenging as it requires a paradigm shift in terms of knowledge production, giving equal recognition to the farmer as a producer of knowledge.

'Lab-to-lab' is reflected in the All India Coordinated Research Projects, in which we brought together scientists working on a particular crop and provided a forum for sharing their knowledge, research and experience—a powerful instrument for the rapid identification of good varieties. In 1965, I convened the All India Coordinated Project on Wheat and involved research institutions in various places, including the agricultural universities at Indore, Pusa, Kanpur, Pantnagar and Ludhiana. This was responsible for the breakthrough in wheat production all over North India.

I have been talking about the Krishi Vigyan Kendras (KVKs). We have nearly 600 now in the country. This is what I call 'lab-to-land' where the KVKs provide the channel for ensuring that research in the labs in agricultural universities or ICAR institutes is tested in and linked to the field. The KVK focuses on learning by doing, not by lecturing, and that is a very effective pedagogic method for the empowerment of people. In setting up new KVKs, I always felt that Kurien's method of sending a 'spearhead' team was useful. I did it when I was managing the KVK in the 1970s. Whenever there was an opportunity, for instance, somebody wanted to give land or facilities for setting up a KVK, we would send a team to understand the context, identify the opportunities, the skills required and so on. This was quite effective.

Even at that time, we set up two KVKs solely for women—one was at Kasturba Gram in Indore and another at Gandhi Ashram in

With Kalaivani Rajendran at the inauguration of the Farmer Field School.

Nagaland. Later on, one more was added at the Avinashalingam Home Science College at Coimbatore. Apart from credible women's organisations, we also identified credible NGOs such as the Ramakrishna Mission at Ranchi, who run an excellent KVK with great dedication and devotion. Unfortunately, after I left ICAR as DG, they stopped giving KVKs to NGOs—these are either given under political pressure or put in agricultural universities. While 'lab-to-lab' and 'lab-to-land' are fairly well established, the other two areas need strengthening.

My idea of 'land-to-land' really implies farmer-to-farmer learning. The first step is the farm school. We find people like Kalaivani Rajendran from Pasupathikovil in Thanjavur, who has been running a very successful Field Training School, sharing information on the SRI (System of Rice Intensification) technique of rice production and the usage of drum seeder for direct sowing (*www.mssrf.org/sites/default/files/Technology%20day_2009_0.pdf*), or Eldho Baby in a small village called Settukkunnu in Wayanad (*The Hindu*, 18 June 2014), experiencing difficulty meeting the demand. Both the Government and donors underestimate the knowledge of the farmers and feel that other farmers will not attend. The main reason the field schools have not spread is the lack of resources. The private sector is not interested in farmer-to-farmer learning, as they want to sell their company's knowledge and seeds. This can however be a very effective way of knowledge transfer, as when one farmer demonstrates something which has worked, and is sustainable, it has much higher credibility, in terms of economics of the technology or practice.

The final one, 'land-to-lab', is the most difficult to implement as it involves learning from indigenous knowledge, a knowledge reversal in some respects. Farmers' wisdom, for example, in medicinal plants is known about, yet we have not taken up testing and validation of this knowledge through scientific methods. It is however gaining attention, with people like Anil Gupta at the Indian Institute of Management, Ahmedabad, maintaining databases of indigenous knowledge and creating spaces for the recognition and reward of grass-roots innovators.

Gender Dimensions of Science and Technology

NR: *Sitting in the audience at MSSRF, Chennai, on 8 March this year, listening to 40 year old Maheshwari, from a fishing village in Puducherry, recount her experiments with cooking, was a direct challenge to the middle class researchers' stereotypes of poor women as victims of male domination. She recounted, "Every time the food is burnt, you know it is my work. I have now given up and handed over to my husband, who does such a good job with the cooking, while I remain preoccupied with my work in the Village Knowledge Centre."*[1] *"My husband is like my friend; he is so understanding," says a soft-spoken Magesh from Nagapattinam. She has a disabled daughter, 12 years old, and let down by both her mother and mother-in-law, she could not have survived without the support of her husband. Another example is Savitha, a Village Knowledge Worker, who went to Geneva for a conference. When asked if she was homesick, she said, "No, I sent an email to my husband every two hours and he replied."*

Listening to these women, I realised that this evidence of transformation in the real lives of very poor women and men has perhaps been the greatest reward for you. Women play a central role in agriculture, yet even today

1. The main aim of the Village Knowledge Centres at MSSRF is to empower largely unskilled, resource-poor rural farming and fishing communities towards making better choices and achieving greater control of their own development through the dissemination of community-centric content developed in a bottom-up manner.

should address the gender dimensions of farming and the issues confronting the small farmer. This will vary across crops and farming systems, but the underlying fact that needs to be recognised is that agriculture has to be an instrument of a sustainable quality of life for the entire family. Different members may have different requirements, which must be addressed. Mina tried to develop a gender curriculum for agricultural universities. Unfortunately, this was never taken up by any agricultural university, not even the one which collaborated with us on developing it! Gender continues to be seen as a personal rather than professional issue.

When we started work in the Kolli Hills in 1994, we found many varieties of millets, and while women knew about their nutritional content, their cultivation was rapidly declining. The main problem was the lack of mechanised milling. Women had to hand pound the millets, which was taking too much time and energy. We got a few machines fabricated and this was appreciated by the local people; however, it was not thereafter taken up either by the Government or any private entrepreneur. As an NGO, we can demonstrate, but replication has to be done either by the state or markets. Perhaps more could also have been done by MSSRF to engage with policy makers so as to convince them of the importance of such technologies and equipment. I spoke about the 'seeing eye and understanding heart'. If these two are absent, you don't see the

Hand pounding millets: Women in Kolli Hills.

realities; women may be doing the work, but this is taken for granted, rather than explicitly recognised.

NR: *Do you think this is a result of institutional cultures within organisations working with farmers?*

MSS: When I was a Trustee of the Ford Foundation (1989-1997), as an equal opportunity Foundation, half the Trustees were women. One of them, Wilma Mankiller, was the leader of the Cherokee tribe in the US. The President of Ford Foundation, Susan Berresford, used to say that it was not a question of man or woman, but by having a diversity of people (by gender, ethnicity, nationality) on the Board of Trustees, different insights into ground realities could be explored. Diversity gives strength, and recognising human diversity can unleash our creative potential.

But these prejudices are deep. When I was President of International Union for Conservation of Nature (IUCN) (1988-1996), I noticed there was only one lady from Ecuador on the Board. At the very first meeting I asked why this was the case, especially as we always talk of women as conservers of biodiversity and protectors of life. Gradually we did expand the number of women members, but the point is that it is not women as women I am talking about, but the recognition that they bring some specialised knowledge and interests to the table, the acknowledgement that we will benefit from diversity. This has happened in Europe where women are in important scientific positions: the Master of Fitzwilliam House in Cambridge and the Director of the Sainsbury Laboratory, they are both women. People accept their leadership, and don't see whether they are women or men. In India, there are very few women Directors of scientific establishments, and only five women have so far been Presidents of the Science Congress over its 100-year history. Even in MSSRF, where we had an almost equal number of men and women in senior positions when we started, this is no longer the case. The prejudice that women can work less because they have responsibilities at home persists across institutions. As a geneticist, I see no inherent differences between men and women; it is the opportunity and encouragement that makes the difference.

I recall that when I joined ICAR, there were no women on the Governing Board and for the first time I brought four women to the Board, one each from Nagaland, Tamil Nadu, UP and Bihar. Fakhrudin Ali Ahmed, who was the then Minister of Agriculture, asked me an interesting question, "Swaminathan, from where did you get all these names, how did you find them?" It was through my own visits, meeting and talking to them; I found them extremely knowledgeable and competent. I don't know how many women are now on the Board; the issue concerns substantially recognising their intellectual contributions, not just physical work as agricultural labourers or domestic workers responsible for bringing fodder, fuel and water.

NR: *Are you hopeful that things might change in the coming years?*

MSS: There is now some pressure from donors such as DFID (Department for International Development of the UK Government) and IDRC (International Development Research Centre, supported by the Canadian Department for Foreign Affairs, Trade and Development) to focus on the gender dimensions and impacts of all research

Training women: Village Knowledge Centre.

programmes. This is however relatively new. In the past, focus has been directed at women, more in terms of affirmative action—number of trustees, number of women scientists and so on—rather than the impact of agricultural research and development on the position of women in society. The women and rice farming programme I started in 1985 as DG, IRRI, was radical for that time, not an accepted practice in the organisation.

What gives me hope is how articulate and confident some of the women with whom we have worked have become. When we introduced the Village Knowledge Centres, I asked Balaji, who developed the programme, to first train women as knowledge workers. If they sit behind the knowledge desk, and men come to them for information, immediately their self-esteem goes up. A central part of the process of empowerment is enhancing their self-esteem and self-confidence, giving them respect as human beings. Today many of the women proudly call themselves Plant Doctors, Academicians, Community Hunger Fighters or Community Climate Risk Managers. They are no longer helpless. We can see both economic and social transformation in these villages.

Youth: Farming in the Future

NR: *The youth and their aspirations has been a key concern for you in relation to the agricultural future of the country. The National Policy of Farmers 2007 clearly defined strategies for attracting and retaining youth, alongside addressing gender inequalities in agriculture. Your emphasis has particularly been on skills, yet this is an area where little action seems to have been taken. What is the way forward?*

MSS: Today, the younger generation of fisher people are very enthusiastic, as they have cell phones and can access various kinds of Global Positioning System (GPS) data on wave heights, fish shoals, and where the Sri Lankan waters start, through the 'fisher-friendly' application in the Nagapattiman-Puducherry coastline of Tamil Nadu. At the same time, we have established a Fish for All Centre at Poompuhar, mainly for women, because once the fish comes to the shore, the women take over further processing, storage and marketing. Given complaints around food safety resulting from poor sanitary

Learning about wave heights: Fisher-friend application.

and phyto-sanitary (measures for control of diseases) conditions for processing fish, we try to impart skills of better management to fisherwomen.

The younger generation are technology-savvy. If we upgrade them technologically, they will find fishing or farming relevant to their own times. Such dynamism in course curriculum and pedagogic methodologies, however, is mostly absent in our educational institutions. The syllabi, once formulated, have hardly been changed to keep pace with generational changes in terms of technology. Use of biotechnology, bioremediation, bio-fortification and other such biological software, alongside some mechanisation, can contribute to improving the efficiency of farming.

In Kerala's Kuttanad region, large areas are reclaimed from the sea for cultivating paddy. Harvesting is still done by women, cutting the paddy by hand with a sickle. Invariably, there are heavy rains in November. The paddy placed on bunds gets soaked and develops mycotoxins.[2] In 2010, based on my report, popularly referred to as the Kuttanad Package, they introduced combine harvesting. The young people took charge, hiring the combine harvesters from Tamil Nadu. Harvesting was completed in 15 days, before the rains came, and the crop could be safely removed from the fields and stored.

A few years ago, when I visited the University of Alberta, I went to see the farms. One farmer had the latest John Deere equipment. He was very proud of it. It was air-conditioned. He gave me the driving wheel, and asked me to try. Within an hour he can harvest 10 acres, but I did one acre because I was going very slowly. But the equipment was impressive—it harvests, threshes, cleans and puts the grain in the silo. That is how they manage. It is a different world of mechanised farming; however, we need to at least semi-mechanise, not only to reduce drudgery, but also to improve efficiency. It is interesting, but also sad, that in a country like India today, we continue to provide unskilled jobs to the poor, but skill is important for the youth.

A second element is management, or what I call the small farm management revolution, that can be brought about by the young people. F.L. Brayne recommended this a long time ago, some form of collective endeavour to provide services and reduce risks. I recommended agri-clinics on the production side in order to control pests, diseases and soil health, and agri-business centres on the post-harvest side. Four or five young agricultural graduates could be encouraged to collectively set up an agri-clinic-cum-agri-business centre in a village. The idea is to provide services such as pest-proofing, for instance, to the rural people for a fee. In the urban areas, there are a lot of service organisations, but none in the rural areas, so young people can fill this gap.

If we take the example of information and communication technologies for villages, there are three possible methods of management: community management, cooperative management and commercial management. The Indian Institute of Technology (IIT) approach led by Ashok Jhunjhunwala follows the STD (Subscribers Trunk Dialling)/ISD (International Subscriber Dialling) model of

2. Mycotoxins are a group of naturally occurring chemicals produced by certain moulds, which can create adverse health effects on human beings.

6

Agricultural Research Strategies

NR: *A partnership with farmers seems very fundamental to your views on agricultural science. At the same time, you have always emphasised originality, creativity and a search for knowledge, rather than repetition and replication. I would like you to spell out how you have developed the various strands of your thinking into a coherent research strategy?*

MSS: One of the greatest challenges before all scientific establishments is what I call sustainable dynamism. While you are dynamic in the beginning, how do you maintain such dynamism in an institution? This can only come from originality in thinking; you can't be stuck with the same problem throughout your life, doing research which is repetitive. When I returned from IRRI and wanted to set up a research institution, MS Swaminathan Research Foundation (MSSRF), everyone thought this would be on rice or wheat or potato—the areas of my personal research that have been globally recognised. But I was clear that I wanted to do something exciting and new, something which filled a gap in ongoing research. Problems of sea level rise and the impact of climate change on coastal systems became a starting point, as no one else was focusing on these issues then. I didn't want yet one more institution for its own sake, but rather one that could fill critical gaps in knowledge.

Further, one needs to be open to mid-course corrections. If something is not working, don't persist with it. Unfortunately, there is resistance to this. People find it comfortable to do what they have always been doing in a rather routine way; they take any feedback as criticism or a failure, rather than positively. This is where good leadership becomes important. In the early years of MSSRF, there were creative young leaders, like V. Balaji and Balasubramanaim, who were very open-minded, had a vision, were dynamic, and most importantly, had a deep commitment to women, the poor and marginalised. They were willing to lead by example, while receptive of new ideas and insights.

In my view, one of the important tasks of science is to help in shaping the future, not merely predicting it. In MSSRF, we have adopted a three-pronged research strategy of anticipatory, participatory and strategic research.

Anticipatory: Responding to New Challenges

NR: *Anticipatory approach seems to be a novel approach for scientific research. Could you explain this a little more?*

MSS: Let me take the example of climate change. It has at least two or three important implications: (a) mean temperature may go up by at least 1.5 degree centigrade; (b) drought and floods, excess or deficient rain may become more common; and (c) the coastal areas will face a problem of sea level rise. These are not conjectures any more. Our anticipatory research agenda must address these issues, providing insights and ideas on what action can be taken to prepare for these changes.

In coastal areas, for instance, the focus can be on developing varieties which are tolerant to sea water, which can withstand floods, and so on. We have excellent varieties of flood-tolerant rice, from what is called the elongation gene, or floating rice. Similarly drought-tolerant varieties can be developed, as we have done using *Prosopis juliflora* as a donor. So one aspect of anticipatory research is to look at the scientific challenges and at the problems of new pests and diseases, what I call the scientific checkmating of potential threats to food security and agriculture.

Stable agriculture requires eternal vigilance. Take, for example, the potato. We produce about 45 million tonnes of potato, an increase from 5 million tonnes recorded 50 years ago. The reason for such a big jump in production was the use of the 'seed plot technique', a method by which seed potato can be produced in the plains of India during the winter months. Earlier we had to get the seeds from the mountains of Himachal Pradesh, Darjeeling or from Nepal. This method enabled the production of potato seeds during seasons when the *Aphid* vector was absent, thereby helping to avoid virus diseases. If the temperature goes up, this advantage maybe lost. If we want to safeguard potato production in the future, then we need to invest in anticipatory research on an alternative method for seed production which is free from viruses.

Similarly in the case of wheat, higher temperatures of 1.5-2 degrees will reduce the duration of the wheat crop by one week. We will have to change the breeding strategy from per crop productivity to per day productivity. We have to select varieties characterised by high per day productivity, because if the crop duration goes down, then the yield too will decrease. The current estimate is that 7-8 million tonnes of wheat will be lost if the temperature goes up by 1.5 degrees because of the shortened duration available for maturation. On the other hand, places like Canada and Siberia will benefit from higher temperatures, because for them the crop duration will increase and so will the yield. We need proactive analysis and action for genetic checkmating of the adverse impact of climate change, and while this is talked about, not much work is being done. There is a climate mission, but their approach is by and large not anticipatory or strategic.

The idea of a mission is that there is a clear goal and one brings all the ingredients together in a strategy to achieve that goal. The word 'mission' was first coined by President John F. Kennedy for landing man on the moon before the end of the 1960s. The decision was political, and he left the rest to his technical teams. Unfortunately, he didn't live to see the day Neil Armstrong landed on the moon in 1968. I was in the United States (US) on that day, with Orville Vogel at Washington State University. We were in the fields, it was August, and the days were long. At around 4 pm, he said, "It is time to go to the house to see the moon-landing." When they landed, the door didn't open for a few minutes and there was tremendous tension. Fortunately, a few minutes later, the door opened and Armstrong came out. That was a really exciting moment. But the point I was trying to make is that we have many missions—the Climate Mission, Nutrition Mission, Pulses Mission—but they don't have a time-bound strategy to achieve these. Today these terms are taken in a very lighthearted way, they have become empty words. The Mission Director has authority, but no accountability to deliver on the promises.

Another important area for anticipatory research relates to market conditions. The monsoon and the market are the two major determinants of farmers' well-being. Today the market is very volatile, so how does one develop more stable prices for agricultural commodities? Last year, our new *Basmati* rice strains from IARI provided ₹30,000 crore (1 crore = 10 million) more income to the farmers, as they are highly valued for their quality in the international market. The investment in this research is a few crores of rupees every year. The returns are huge—this is the power of science. Quality is crucial.

We have a long coastline but our fish products are often infected with *salmonella*; this year our *Alfonso* mango has been banned from European markets due to pesticide residues. While there is good work done on *basmati* as well as wheat varieties, nobody is working on quality and safety issues for other agricultural products. There needs to be a purpose and a philosophy underlying the research strategy: either to stabilise production, to increase incomes, or to improve farmers' well-being. Unfortunately, the research leadership by and large today does not have a clear purpose or strategy.

Strategic Research: Original Thinking

NR: *You have always seen challenges as opportunities for original thinking. While the core sciences often engage with strategic research, this seems to have been less common in the field of agriculture. Can you explain why this might be the case?*

MSS: If we want to shape the future, not follow it, we need to look at problems strategically. When I was first thinking about our research agenda at MSSRF in 1989, I organised a meeting with key people at the Indian Institute of Technology (IIT) in Chennai. They were surprised that I should talk about preparing for sea level rise. In those days, climate change was not a big issue; we were much ahead of the time. Fortunately, I was invited by the Japanese government to give a talk in Tokyo. Dr Saburo Okita, former Foreign Minister of Japan, who

Halophyte garden, Vedaranyam.

received the Magsaysay award the same year as I did (1971), chaired my lecture on the preparation for sea level rise. Since Japan is a country of islands, he felt that this was an area which required support, so he offered half a million dollars from the Japanese government to MSSRF, routed through the International Tropical Timber Organisation (ITTO). That is how we started our work on mangroves as a way of addressing sea level rise. We had a very good team of young scientists like Rajeshwari Anand (the then Mahalingam), Sanjay Deshmukh and Hemal Kanvinde. Balaji joined at that time and set up our Informatics programme, the Village Knowledge Centres. This was 25 years ago, much before the ICT (information and communication technology) boom in India.

Once the purpose is clear, strategic research may involve both conventional technologies and frontier technologies. Conventional technologies include normal Mendelian breeding, for instance: one can do a lot of selection in the coastal areas from mangrove crops or halophytes. These have hardly been studied, hence we have set up a genetic garden of halophytes near Vedaranyam in order to collect

htm). For me, participatory research is different. First of all, it is about enabling farmers to develop their own varieties. For instance, we do the pre-breeding, say, taking the genes for salt tolerance from a halophyte. We give this to the farmers to transfer to their own local varieties. They can do it very well. I call 'every farmer a scientist', as agriculture in the future will be more and more knowledge-intensive, not capital or chemical-intensive, and will also be eco-system specific.

A second dimension of participatory research is the possibility of combining ecological prudence, traditional wisdom and practical experiences of the communities with modern science. If we recognise that the breeder, the farmer and the forester are all allies in the same struggle, it will be a win-win for sustainable agriculture. The Gulf of Mannar was one of the Biosphere Reserves recognised by the United Nations Educational, Scientific and Cultural Organization (UNESCO) as a globally important biological site. The Gulf of Mannar consists of 21 islands with numerous beautiful crustaceans, flora and fauna—most of it, unfortunately, severely depleted. We wanted to revive the Gulf of Mannar Biosphere in collaboration with the local communities, mainly fishermen, those living on sea and marine products like agar agar, corals and so on. I felt that the only way this could be done was by forming a Trust, where the property is held in trust by the local community as well as government departments, mainly Forestry and Fisheries. Here, Gandhiji's idea of trusteeship became the method of managing the biosphere, giving explicit recognition to the local communities. One should not consider oneself as the owner of wealth, but hold it in trust for the future generations. Jamsetji Tata once wrote, "Give back to society what you have taken from them"—and that is how the Tata Trusts were formed. So trusteeship implies ownership for public good rather than for private profit. In fact, it was this concept that made me use all the money that I had received in the form of various prizes for public good research through the Foundation, rather than keeping it for my personal use.

The Gulf of Mannar project was supported by the Global Environment Facility. Unfortunately, once the funding was over, it has gone back to the Forest Department and they manage it in their own way. By and large, they are unable to shift their attitudes towards

the community and adopt a truly participatory approach. The social mobilisation was also not strong enough to ensure that the community groups kept up pressure from below. The Gulf of Mannar Biosphere Trust has once again become the 'Gulf of Mannar Biosphere Reserve'. It is not enough to temporarily give voice to communities, they also need to be organised to ensure that they retain their rights and are able to exercise their responsibilities.

A third area relates to genuine participatory consultation before taking any major decisions. Manas National Park in Bodoland, Assam, is a world heritage site, but it was being destroyed. When I visited there along with the then Director of the Park, the late Sanjoy Deb-Roy, in 1989, the Bodos said:

> We are told that it is a World Heritage site, but this is our heritage, not the Forest Department's heritage. Our ancestors built this sanctuary, but someone else has gone to UNESCO, Paris, and enlisted us as a heritage site without our knowledge, consent or any consultation.

This lack of communication led to the conflict between the tribal families and the foresters—each blaming the other for destroying the forests. When we were planning to propose the Kuttanad below sea-level farming as a Globally Important Agricultural Heritage System (GIAHS), the first thing I did was to write to the Chief Minister of Kerala and the local farmers' associations, called Padasekhara Samithis, asking for their views. They realised it would give recognition to the innovative capacity of the farmers of Kuttanad and welcomed the move.

Research, I feel, should ultimately contribute towards empowerment of the rural population, both men and women, and an improvement in their quality of life. From this perspective, we need to anticipate the challenges and risks of the future, and develop strategies collaboratively with those whose lives we want to touch.

7

Science and Public Policy

NR: *The strong prejudice that we still have against the tribal communities in the country often strikes me. We give tribals recognition only for their physical work, as clearers of forests or hard-working labour, but not for their skills or intellect. I was very moved when a group of educated young tribal boys and girls in Jharkhand expressed their frustration about the National Rural Employment Guarantee Scheme (NREGS). While acknowledging its role in social protection, they were disappointed that though they were educated and had skills, the only employment available to them even now was unskilled manual labour.*

During the late 1980s, with the start of the literacy campaigns, the People's Science Movement gained ground across the country. I was involved with some of the campaigns in Tamil Nadu which used a range of communication methods, from literacy primers to street theatre (kala jathas), to challenge superstitions and prejudices. You spoke earlier about the political and public understanding of science. I wanted to ask you not just about your more recent political engagement, but also about the ways you have engaged with other public stakeholders, including building scientific curiosity and understanding amongst children and in communities.

Developing a Scientific Temper

NR: *Could you tell me a little about your own efforts to develop a scientific temperament amongst farmers and communities, especially young people?*

MSS: As Jawaharlal Nehru frequently emphasised, the creation of a scientific temper in the country is absolutely essential for progress of the nation, both scientific and economic, as this removes many superstitious beliefs and prejudices. This is particularly important in our country, where we have a diversity of languages, religions, communities, castes and economic conditions, and more so in agriculture, which employs over 60 per cent of the population. I am a geneticist and believe that some knowledge of genetics, of the human genome and of chromosomes, can help explain certain characteristics and behaviours of a person; this has nothing to do with one's caste or religion. People should understand that our genetic heritage is common.

The growth of a scientific temper has to start from a young age, only then can prejudices based on caste and religion be removed. We started a programme at MS Swaminathan Research Foundation (MSSRF) called 'Every Child a Scientist' about 15 years ago. This was really a programme started in the US by Bruce Alberts when he was President of the US National Academy of Sciences (1993-2005). I thought it was an excellent idea; it is not about introduction to a scientific career, but rather developing a questioning mind, where irrational prejudices are not accepted as the truth.

Our aim was to focus on children from the underprivileged municipality schools. We talk to them about biodiversity and human diversity, of diversity as strength rather than weakness, and hence

Every child a scientist: Summer programme.

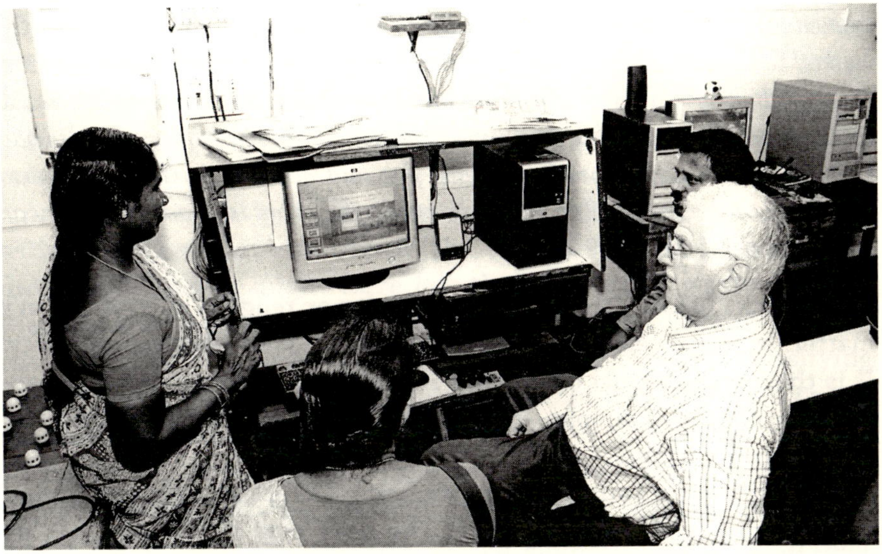

Bruce Alberts at a Village Knowledge Centre

why it should not become a basis for prejudices, discrimination and conflicts. The children's programme has gone very well and the Department of Biotechnology has now extended it across the country. Special four-week courses and trips are organised for children by NGOs (non-governmental organisations) in different parts of the country during the summer holidays to biodiversity-rich areas, exposing them to biodiversity and its conservation as well as the significance of genome studies. It is unfortunate that such science education is not being imparted through our formal educational institutions.

Apart from children, the question of scientific temper is also important amongst adults. In our work in tribal areas, we have discussed with the communities about the extraordinary biodiversity even within their own context, and the sharing of knowledge, for instance, of medicinal plants, what I call curative diversity, from one community to the other.

NR: *The other day a friend of mine who was staying in the MSSRF guest house told me something interesting. He was sitting in the canteen when a large number of labourers who were working in the compound*

the Indian freedom movement, and also the last Governor-General of India) spoke against going by horoscopes in fixing marriages, giving several examples of how even careful matching can result in unfortunate events.

Mina: One of the great surprises is that you find people who are superstitious at both ends of the spectrum. This includes scientists. For example, there are jokes about one of our leading scientists, who was Head of the National Physical Laboratory in the 1960s. He had a great name in science, but was very particular about rituals and *muhurthams*. I don't think this kind of superstitious thinking is part of the Hindu religion; rather it is the belief that religion has to be performed through rituals. Today you find more and more of these —numerology and adding letters to one's name is an example. I think what Appa finds hard to imagine is how people are able to lead their life in compartments, one segment of the brain believes in this and another segment of the brain in something else. Scientists also consult astrologers. When we got married, my parents wrote to his uncle, M.K. Narayanswami (Kunchappa) saying, "The young people have decided to marry. We don't believe in horoscopes, but if you wish, please go ahead and consult the horoscopes." Kunchappa refused. Later my mother-in-law explained it to me, saying, "Supposing we had found that the horoscopes didn't match, it would only lead to pain, discomfort and unnecessary tension, so why have that?" It was a very practical and pragmatic approach, and I think women are much more practical, as they are the ones who have to manage the everyday tasks and relationships.

Communicating Science

NR: *Apart from the gap between belief and practice, there is a second issue which relates to the responsibility for communication. You mentioned the importance of the public understanding of science, but how far do you feel scientists give attention to communication with the public, to going beyond scientific publications?*

MSS: Science communication to various stakeholders is very important because it is easy to both misinterpret and misuse science.

We need to think about the use and abuse of science separately from the science itself. Take, for example, nuclear power; you can create clean energy or you can make atomic bombs; there is also a lot of apprehension and fear that nuclear power is dangerous following Chernobyl, Fukushima and several other accidents. But nuclear power is environmentally benign, as is hydro-power, while fossil fuels contribute to climate change. Clearly there are trade-offs, one needs to give adequate attention to issues of safety, to local forest-based livelihoods, before moving ahead. Similar is the case of biotechnology; there is a lot of apprehension about genetic engineering, but it also provides uncommon opportunities for creating novel genetic combinations. The issue confronting the scientist is how to carefully examine the risks and benefits and present a balanced account to the political leaders and also the public. Risks should not be understated and benefits overstated. An independent, regulatory mechanism often becomes essential in such circumstances.

One problem in our country seems to relate to science communication. Often scientists speak only in English, or they have a particular manner of speaking and language that is not easily understandable to the lay person. Even in MSSRF, most of the scientists publish only in scientific journals, not in the popular media. There are several methods of communication, some are direct, like lab-to-land or Farmer Field Schools, but we need to be aware that there are other stakeholders too, and we need to communicate with them, whether middle class consumers or policy makers.

In an area like GM (genetically modified) foods, the oppositional movements are able to communicate well with the consumers and create a fear psychosis, while the scientists are unable to get their point across. Recently, in the Philippines, fields of Golden Rice (GM), acclaimed for being rich in Vitamin A, were burnt by the public. Such confrontation can only be overcome by effective communication and open debate; it is not enough to say, "Don't be afraid of the technology." Communication skills are poor and communication needs are not understood; the timing and the language of communication, these are all very important. That is why I have recommended on many occasions that Indian Council of Agricultural Research (ICAR) and other scientific institutions should have media resource centres through which scientific facts can be easily communicated in the local languages by the media to the wider public. Scientific establishments have not really paid any attention to media relations in India.

Take another example, that of subsidies. The Punjab government provided a subsidy to ensure free electricity for all farmers. I called this ecological suicide as the water-table was already going down, and this subsidy led to even more depletion due to over-drawing and over-use of water, leading ultimately to soil salinity. This was not needed at all to maintain crop yields; in fact, too much water can harm the crop. But the Green Revolution is blamed, rather than the public policy measure, which had been a populist election promise. Most important, I think, is the openness towards sharing information, discussing issues, and communicating effectively the risks and gains. Daisoku Ikeda, the well-known Buddhist leader, often says that many of the problems of the world can be resolved through conversation—the more people converse with each other, the more misunderstandings are removed. There is no harm in admitting one doesn't know something; after all, we are learning throughout our life, but we should not mislead people by holding back information or refusing to discuss problematic areas.

Mina: I wanted to add a little about the effects of the educational system and the language in which you learn. Science is learnt in English, but you learn certain other things in your own languages and hence each inhabits a different region of the mind, a different consciousness. English is important, but it shapes a different way of thinking and understanding; hence many scientists don't have the concepts or vocabulary to explain and express their ideas, especially about science, in their own language. The two contexts are different; that is why our scientists, for instance, can't understand the alternate way of thinking of the rural poor.

Spending time with people is another way of understanding different forms of thinking and talking. For example, in Tamil, and this is true of all Indian languages, people speak largely in analogies and comparative terms; they rarely give you direct answers to a question. It is an oblique use of language, but equally gives due consideration to multiple outcomes and possibilities, in contrast to scientific language which is both direct and linear. I have once seen, in response to a rather knotty problem, the elder present simply responded by saying that when a tree falls, everybody has to join to move it. The community seemed quite satisfied with the answer, and dispersed, though there was no tree nearby! What he meant was that people needed to get together to solve the problem, there was no other way.

The third point is really about information-sharing *versus* communication. The former is one way, giving people information on wave heights, market prices, or whatever else they find useful. But this still doesn't involve two-way communication or interaction, where they can ask questions, you can listen to their ideas, and have a forum for discussion. Different strategies can be used for this purpose. Of course, this requires inter-disciplinary cooperation, and unfortunately as MSSRF has grown, even here people are divided by their disciplinary boundaries, and hardly interact with each other. But for this kind of communication to take place, there has to be some investment of time and effort to create suitable fora; it will not happen automatically. If you look at the MSSRF website, for instance, mostly Appa contributes news items, and perhaps a few others.

Sustained Engagement with Policy

NR: *You had a lot of success with policy engagement in the 60s and 70s, in fact you attribute the success of the yield revolution to this 'symphony' between scientists, policy-makers and farmers. While this seems to have broken down over the last decade, you have tried, even in your personal capacity, to ensure that innovative ideas reach the government and policy-makers, first through the National Farmers' Commission and later the Rajya Sabha. While you were officially appointed to these positions of authority, the ideas you presented have not been picked up by policy. What do you think are the reasons for this?*

MSS: The National Commission on Farmers was set up in 2004. Most previous Commissions were for farming, not farmers; here the idea was to put faces before figures. We submitted the final report within two years—a record for a Commission of this kind (*http://*

At a meeting of the National Farmers' Commission.

www.kisanayog.gov.in/). In fact, I decided to split it into shorter reports, so that money could be provided in the interim budgets for implementation. Five reports were submitted, and these have been universally acclaimed. Unfortunately no action has been taken by the Ministry of Agriculture.

I am not able to say exactly why no action was taken; maybe one or two recommendations went against the interests of bureaucrats, as we had recommended that the Ministry should be professionalised, and key positions occupied by outstanding farmers who understand rural realities and the problems confronting farmers today. Another, I think, is the difference in world views: I firmly believe that public good research and extension need to remain in the public sector and be strengthened, as it is only this that can make it inclusive and contribute to equitable outcomes. The mainstream trend within the Government, however, seems to favour the private sector and profit motive. An important recommendation that has not been implemented was that the procurement price of wheat or rice should be C2 (that is, total cost of production plus 50%). I thought this was essential to lift small farmers above the poverty line—they need a reasonable income.

Based on the report, however, we drafted a National Policy for Farmers. This was endorsed by the Ministers of Agriculture of different states and was approved by the Parliament in 2007, after I joined the Rajya Sabha. I had suggested that a day's time be allocated for discussing this policy and the report, given the agrarian crisis facing the country, and the spate of farmer suicides. The Government however, did not want any debate on the subject. Venkaiah Naidu of the Bharatiya Janata Party (BJP), and D. Raja of Communist Party of India (CPI) occasionally raised the issue in the Parliament, but soon it was forgotten.

So politics can be a very powerful ally for science and for scientific progress, but it can also become an impediment, leading to frustration when you can't do much. If the Farmers' Commission report had been acted upon, it would have changed the face of farmers and farming in India. Clearly this is not what the political class of today wants, unlike Nehru, Shastri and Subramaniam. There seems to be an interest in maintaining power differentials between the rural and the urban, between farmers and service providers.

The second area which was not acted on was Report of the Committee on Biotechnology set up in 2003 during the Vajpayee government, of which I was the Chair. We recommended a Parliament-approved Biotechnology Regulatory Authority, which could carefully examine risks and benefits of all new biotechnologies from the perspective of bio-safety, allaying apprehensions of NGOs and the public. The report was released officially after Sharad Pawar took office as Minister of Agriculture in 2004, but this also has not been acted upon; with the result that between 2004 and 2014, we have not set up a proper regulatory mechanism, except one within the Ministry of Environment, chaired by an Additional Secretary. An opportunity for significant anticipatory research has been lost. More recently, a Supreme Court Committee has recommended that no field trials with

I wanted to use this opportunity to ensure the entitlements of women farmers in this country. After discussions with many NGOs, academics, political parties and legal experts, I placed the Women Farmer's Entitlement Bill (2011) in the Rajya Sabha in May 2012 (*http://kractivist.files.wordpress.com/2012/06/women-farmers-bill-2012_english.pdf*). Unfortunately, till the end of my term, in March 2013, I did not get an opportunity to formally introduce the Bill, which lapsed with the end of my term in the Parliament. This remains a regret; I was unable to influence the political class to change their attitudes towards farmers in general and women farmers in particular. Perhaps the clash with the dominant worldview was too strong.

Reflections

My parents left Norwich early in the morning, on the May 29 2014. I would have liked them to stay longer, but he had to go to New Delhi for important meetings with the newly elected Prime Minister and other officials the next day. From there, he would go on to Chennai, and I don't know where else. As children, I recalled, we used to joke that we didn't ever know where he was: one day in Indore for a training camp in hand-pollination for women; back to Delhi for a day, and then on to Hanoi, or Rome, or Mexico City. He would go on tirelessly. A speech here, an inauguration there, a few words of encouragement to a student at an airport, or asking a chauffeur driving him from Indore to Bhopal, whether his wife had recovered from her illness, though they had last met two years ago. He is my father, and I am proud of him. The lines of the Sanskrit verse, Charaiveti, Charaiveti, from the Aitareya Brahmanam of the Rig Veda (7.15) kept churning in my head after they left.[1]

Charaiveti, Charaiveti. The Buddha concluded his discourses and sermons with these words: move on, move on. Change is the only permanence in life. Sometimes change can exhilarate and excite, sometimes it can frustrate and demoralise. And change can be scary and terrifying. Remembering his stories of growing up without a father since the age of 11, and considering his present schedules, all I could tell myself was: No matter how arduous the climb, how long and winding the road, how worn out we are, we need to carry on, keep going, as long as we can. This movement is not just about the physical, but about the creativity and adaptability of ideas to changing contexts. Indifferent to praise or criticism, he has a definite purpose, a clear direction, a strong ethical stance in favour of equity and justice, as a voice for farmers, men and women, often unseen and unheard. This seems to be the essential philosophy of his life and work.

1. *Charan vai madhu vindati, Charan swadum udumbaram. Suryasya pasya shremanam, Yo na tandrayate charan. Charaiveti, Charaiveti.*
Moving persons get nectar, moving persons get tasty food. See the greatness of the Sun which is never tired of moving. Keep moving, Keep moving.

There has been a shift in his own perspectives, from a focus on sustainable agriculture, to the sustainability of farming livelihoods and farmers' well-being. This is in keeping with one of his favourite sayings—"Putting faces before figures."' I know from our conversations that he also believes in Einstein's dictum: 'We can't solve problems by using the same kind of thinking we used when we created them'; he is always coming up with new ideas, seeing opportunities in every difficulty and still excited when confronted with new challenges.

Perhaps I have been somewhat eulogistic in this round of conversations. Like all mortals, he has several weaknesses; indeed, some of them, like seeing only the good in everyone, which the family often laughs about, have at times led to his being exploited by others! But, he does believe that it's only a life lived for others that is worth living, judging others not by their vices and faults, but by their virtues.

This August, it was his 89th birthday. Despite needing to use a walking stick, he was front and centre of a major international conference, raising the issues confronting resource-poor farmers, with the same enthusiasm as ever and in his own unique style. Charaiveti Charaiveti, Appa.

Afterword

Mina Swaminathan

The 60 years covered by this narrative have been a period of changing world views globally. Particularly after 1989, with the collapse of the Soviet Union and the end of the Cold War, the capitalist ethic of every man (woman) for himself (herself) has become predominant world-wide. Even China is practising state capitalism, with a communist overlay.

In India, this new approach, now more attractively termed neo-liberalism and signalled most clearly in 1991, has grown stronger with each passing year. Whichever government may be in power, India is now unmistakably on the neo-liberal path. This is also painfully reflected in the slow decline, and now electoral demise, of left-oriented parties and politics.

At this point of time in India, then, what do we make of MSS—a scientist loved by the Indian nation for his contribution to national food security and sovereignty—for his constant insistence on public good, public research and public policy, especially in relation to science and agriculture? What do we make of his adherence to Gandhian values at a time when these are widely held to be moribund, though that is rarely acknowledged in public? (Here I must confess that I myself have always been more a Socialist than a Gandhian, but that has never been an obstacle to a harmonious marriage.)

Is he then a dinosaur, past his sell-by date? Or rather, is he, like that other timeless character in a timeless Indian epic, a reminder to the 21st century Indian, carrying the message of a relevant *dharma*?

References

Bauer, P.T. (1981). "The Population Explosion: Myths and Realities", in *Equality, the Third World and Economic Delusion*. Cambridge, Massachusetts: Harvard University Press.

Bernardo, Fernando A. (2010). *50 Years of Progress: Fighting Poverty and Hunger*. Manila, Philippines: IRRI-Philippines. p.366.

Bhoothalingam, S. (1993). *Reflections on an Era*. Madras: Affiliated East-West Press Pvt. Ltd. pp.107-08.

Brayne, F.L. (1929). *Socrates in an Indian Village*. London. Oxford University Press.

Carney, J.P. (2014). "Science Advocacy, Defined", *Science*. 345(6194): 243, 18 July.

Chandrasekhar (2012). "India's Triumph in Rice", *The Hindu*, 23 December

Condorcet on Human Progress (1995). *Population and Development Review* 21(1): 153-61.

Ehrlich, Paul R. (1968). *The Population Bomb*. New York: Ballantine Books.

Government of India (2006). *Report of the Sub-Committee on More Crop and Income per Drop of Water.* New Delhi: Ministry of Water Resources. p.57.

Howard, H.W. and M.S. Swaminathan (1952). "Species Differentiation in the Section Tuberarium, Genus Solanum With Particular Reference to the Use of Interspecific Hybridization in Breeding", *Euphytica* 1: 31-49.

Nature (1972). "How Not to Run Research Councils (Indian Style)", *Nature* 237(5351): 123, 19 May.

Paddock, W. and P. Paddock (1967). *Famine 1975! America's Decision: Who Will Survive?*. London: Little, Brown & Co.

Pandher, S. (2014). "Punjab Shortlists Monsanto, Two Others to Provide Subsidised HYV Maize Seeds", *The Hindu*, 27 May.

Planning Commission (2007). *Recommendations of Working Group on Agricultural Extension for Formulation of Eleventh Five-Year Plan (2007-12)*. New Delhi: Government of India.

Pritchard, B., A. Anu Rammohan, M. Sekher, S. Parasuraman and C. Choithani (2013). *Feeding India: Livelihoods, Entitlements and Capabilities*. London and New York: Earthscan from Routledge.

Puckridge, Don (2004). *The Burning of the Rice: A Cambodian Success Story*. Victoria, USA: Temple House Publishing. p.326.

Sukhatme, P.V. (1965). *Feeding India's Growing Millions*. Bombay: Asia Publishing House.

Swaminathan, M.S. (1953). "Studies on the Inter-relationships Between Taxonomic Series in the Section Tuberarium, Genus Solanum. I. Commersoniana and Tuberosa", *American Potato Journal* 30: 271-81.

———. (1968) *Five Years of Research on Dwarf Wheats.* New Delhi: Indian Agricultural Research Institute.

———. (2013). *From Bengal Famine to Right to Food. The Hindu.* 23 February.

———. (2013a). *Genesis and Growth of the Yield Revolution in Wheat in India: Lessons for Shaping Our Agricultural Destiny.* Agricultural Research. Published online 23 June 2013, doi 10.1007/s40003-013-0069-3.

———. (2014a). "Managing the Monsoon", *The Hindu*, 2 May.

———. (2014b). "A Close Friend of Science", *The Week* 32(20): 94-95.

The Economist (1979). "The Famine That Might Have Been", *The Economist,* 20 October.

The International Rice Research Institute (1985). *Women in Rice Farming: Proceedings of a Conference on Women in Rice Farming Systems.* Manila, Philippines. p.531.

Watson, J.D. and F. H.C Crick (1953). "The Molecular Structure of Nucleic Acids", *Nature* 171(4356): 737-38. (*http://www.nature.com/nature/dna50/watsoncrick.pdf*)

Voelcker, J.A. (1893). *Report on the Improvement of Indian Agriculture.* London: Eyre and Spottiswoode.

References to People

Fakhruddin Ali Ahmed (late), an active Congressman, held several Ministerial portfolios including that of Agriculture before being appointed as the fifth President of India from 1974 to 1977.

Bruce Alberts, Emeritus Professor, University of California at San Francisco, former Editor, *Science*.

Rajeshwari Anand (nee Mahalingam), former project leader of coastal systems research at MSSRF, now runs the Resource Center for Ecohappiness in Arizona as an educational outreach programme.

Neil A. Armstrong (late), an American astronaut and the first person to walk on the Moon. He was also an aerospace engineer, naval aviator, test pilot and university professor.

Charlotte Auerbach (late), a German-Jewish zoologist and geneticist, contributed to founding the science of mutagenesis. She became well known after 1942 for her discovery that mustard gas could cause mutations in fruit flies.

V. Balaji, set up the Informatics Centre at MSSRF, presently Director, Technology and Knowledge Management, Commonwealth of Learning, Canada.

K. Balasubramaniam, Head, Ecotechnology Programme, MSSRF, presently Education Specialist, Agriculture and Livelihoods, Commonwealth of Learning, Canada.

Surjit Singh Barnala, former Chief Minister of Punjab, Governor of Tamil Nadu, Uttarakhand and Andhra Pradesh, served as Union Agriculture Minister in the late 1970s.

Susan Berresford, President of Ford Foundation from 1996 to 2007, she is now a philanthropy consultant.

S. Bhoothalingam (late), ICS, retired as Finance Secretary to Government of India in 1966.

Norman E. Borlaug (late), an American biologist, humanitarian and Nobel laureate; known for developing semi-dwarf, high-yielding, disease-resistant wheat varieties.

F.L. Brayne (late), civil servant, Deputy Commissioner of Gurgaon in the early 1920s, known as the author of *Socrates in an Indian Village*.

V. L. Chopra, Geneticist, retired as DG, ICAR, and Member, Planning Commission.

John Crawford (late), a leading Australian public servant, he played a foundational role in the establishment of the Australian Development Assistance Agency, Consultative Group on International Agricultural Research and others.

C. Dakshinamurthy, formerly Head, Department of Agricultural Physics, IARI.

Sanjoy Debroy (late), Director of the Manas Tiger Reserve, Assam, he retired as Inspector General of Forests (Wildlife), Ministry of Environment and Forests.

Sanjay V. Deshmukh, established MSSRF's programme on coastal systems research. He is currently Professor of Life Sciences at the University of Mumbai.

Venkatrao Gadwal, past President, IARI Students' Union, now Adviser Mahyco.

Annex 1

Farewell Statement by Prof M.S. Swaminathan

22 March 2013

Mr Chairman,

I thank you for this opportunity to make a brief statement at the end of my term as a Nominated Member of the Rajya Sabha. The last six years have helped me to understand the strengths of our Parliamentary Democracy rooted in a Pan-political commitment to secularism and socially inclusive and environmentally sustainable economic growth. My thanks go to you, Mr Chairman as well as the Vice Chairman and the Panel of Chairs for the opportunity you have been giving to Nominated Members to express their views. My sincere thanks also go to the Secretary General and officers of the Secretariat for their unstinted help and guidance whenever needed. I wish to thank the Prime Minister and the Government for choosing an Agricultural Scientist to serve in this House, since this has happened only once before. It has been a privilege sitting on this bench for six years in the company of very distinguished colleagues.

Among the highlights of my tenure in this House, I consider the opportunity to vote in favour of the Bill to reserve one-third of the seats in Parliament for women (Constitution [96th Amendment] Act 2010) as the most important one. I do hope that the Lok Sabha will also pass this Bill soon, so that socio-political empowerment of women, which started at the local body level, can extend to the highest decision-making bodies of our democracy. The current mood in the country favours the speedy end of all forms of gender inequality and injustice.

In life, pleasure and pain go together. While the issue-based support extended by all parties to important pieces of legislation gave me happiness, I feel sorry that my Private Member's Bill entitled the Women Farmers Entitlements Bill, 2011, could not come up for discussion before the end of my term. On two occasions it was listed for discussion, but unfortunately on both the occasions, the proceedings were disrupted, leading to adjournment of the House. I hope soon a consensus will emerge among leaders of political parties that both the Question Hour and the time allotted to Private Members' Business should be out of bounds in relation to disruption.

I request Members to take up the cause of women farmers or *mahila kisans*, who constitute the majority of women in our country, in the interest of both household livelihood security and national food security. In the latest Gender Inequality Index by United Nations Development Programme (UNDP), we occupy the 132nd position among 148 countries. This is a sad situation and without attention to the problems of rural women, we may not be able to improve our position in the area of gender equity.

Another disappointment is poor implementation of the National Policy for Farmers, placed on the table of this House in November 2007. The sooner we change our mindset regarding farm women and men and re-designate for this purpose the Ministry of Agriculture as the "Ministry of Agriculture and Farmers' Welfare", the greater will be the prospects for the country to sustain with home grown food the legal right to food enshrined in the National Food Security Bill. The year 2013 marks the 70th anniversary of the Bengal famine and we should be proud of the fact that our farmers and scientists have enabled us to come out of the ship-to-mouth existence of the 1960s, and initiate the world's largest social protection measure against hunger.

Sir, finally, as a biologist, I wish to cite an outstanding example of democracy at the household level.

All here are aware of the path-breaking work of Charles Darwin in elucidating the origin of species, including ourselves, through evolution. Darwin's wife, Emma, was a staunch Catholic and the theory of evolution was considered blasphemy both to Catholics and several other religious groups at that time. She was once asked how she managed to live peacefully with Charles considering that his theory of evolution was unacceptable to her. She replied, "Charles lives by reason and I live by faith; what leads to faith is feeling and not reasoning. We agree to disagree and live happily together."

"Agreeing to disagree and living happily together" is the very essence of democracy. I am confident that this House will always uphold this principle and thereby remain the flagship of our secular democratic republic.

— M.S. Swaminathan
22 March 2013

M.S. Swaminathan

Highlights of Career

Birth: 7 August, 1925, Kumbakonam, Tamil Nadu.

Education:

- BSc, University of Travancore, 1944.
- BSc, Agriculture from Coimbatore Agricultural College, Madras University, 1947.
- Associate IARI in Genetics, Indian Agricultural Research Institute (IARI), 1947-1949.
- UNESCO Fellow in Genetics at the Agricultural University at Wageningen, The Netherlands, 1949-50.
- PhD from the School of Agriculture, University of Cambridge, UK, in 1952.
- Research Associate in Genetics at the University of Wisconsin, USA, during 1952-53.

Key Positions:

- Teacher and Researcher, Indian Agricultural Research Institute, New Delhi (1954-1966).
- Director, IARI (1966-1972).
- Director General, Indian Council of Agricultural Research (ICAR), and Secretary to the Government of India, Department of Agricultural Research and Education (1972-1979).
- Principal Secretary to the Government of India, Ministry of Agriculture and Irrigation (1979-80).
- Member (Agriculture, Rural Development, Science and Education), Planning Commission, Government of India (1980-1982).

- Director General, International Rice Research Institute (IRRI), Philippines (1982-1988).
- Chairman, M.S. Swaminathan Research Foundation (1989-2012).
- Chairman, National Commission on Farmers, Government of India (2004-2006).
- Member of Parliament (Rajya Sabha) (2007-2013).
- Member, National Advisory Council, Government of India (2010-2012).
- Founder Chairman and Chief Mentor, M.S. Swaminathan Research Foundation (2012 onwards).

Recognition by Science Academies:

- Fellow, Indian National Science Academy (1961).
- Fellow, Royal Society of London (1973).
- Fellow, US National Academy of Sciences (1976).
- Fellow, Russian Academy (1977).
- Fellow, Chinese Academy of Agriculture Sciences (1987).
- President, National Academy of Agricultural Sciences (1991-1996 and 2005-2007).

International Positions Held:

- Independent Chairman, Food and Agriculture Organization (FAO) Council (1981-1985).
- President, World Conservation Union (IUCN) (1984-1990).
- President, Pugwash Conferences on Science and World Affairs (2002-2007).
- Chairman, High Level Panel of Experts on Food Security and Nutrition of the UN Committee on Food Security (CFS), Rome (2010 onwards).

Selected National and International Awards:

- Shanti Swarup Bhatnagar Award for contributions to Biological Sciences (1961).
- Padma Shri (1967).
- Ramon Magsaysay Award for Community Leadership (1971).
- Padma Bhushan (1972).
- Borlaug Award (1979).
- Founding Fellow, Third World Academy of Sciences (1983).
- First International Award of the International Association for Women and Development (1985).
- Albert Einstein World Science Award by the World Cultural Council (1986).
- The Golden Heart Presidential Award of the Philippines (1987).
- First World Food Prize (1987).
- Padma Vibushan (1989).
- The Tyler Prize for Environmental Achievement (1991).
- Honda Prize for Ecotechnology, Tokyo, Japan (1991).
- United Nations Environment Programme (UNEP) - Sasakawa Environment Prize (1994).
- Blue Planet Prize (with MSSRF) (1996).
- Volvo Environment Prize (1999).
- Indira Gandhi Prize for Peace, Disarmament and Development (2000).
- Sahametrei Medal of the Government of Cambodia (2006).

Recognition by Universities:

- Honorary DSc Degree from 70 universities in India and abroad.